So you really want to le

English

2nd Edition

Book Two

Susan Elkin

Series Editor: Nicholas Oulton M.A. (Oxon.)

GALORE PARK

www.galorepark.co.uk

Published by ISEB Publications, an imprint of Galore Park Publishing Ltd
19/21 Sayers Lane, Tenterden, Kent TN30 6BW
www.galorepark.co.uk

Illustrations by Rowan Barnes-Murphy

Design and layout by Qué, Wittersham

Printed by Lego S.p.A., Italy

ISBN: 978 1 905735 62 4

First published 2005, new edition September 2012

An Answer Book is available to accompany this book
ISBN: 978 1 905735 68 6

Details of other Galore Park publications are available at www.galorepark.co.uk

ISEB Revision Guides, publications and examination papers may also be obtained from Galore Park.

The publishers are grateful to the following for permission to use the extracts included in this book:

'Circus Lion' from *Complete Poems of C. Day Lewis* by Cecil Day Lewis, published by Stanford University Press. Reprinted by permission of The Random House Group Ltd and SLL/Sterling Lord Literistic, Inc. (Copyright by C. Day Lewis); 'Retirement for Britain's last performing elephant' Sunday Mirror article, © Sunday Mirror 2011; 'Death of an Aircraft', from *Collected Poems of Charles Causley*, published by Macmillan and reprinted by permission of David Higham Associates; 'Review on a staged production of Lord if the Flies', reprinted by kind permission of *The Stage* newspaper; *Noughts and Crosses* by Malorie Blackman, published by Corgi books. Reprinted by permission of The Random House Group Ltd; 'Telephone Conversation' by Wole Soyinka, reprinted with permission of Melanie Jackson Agency, LLC, NY; extract from Martin Luther King Jr speech, (permission sought); 'Christmas' from *Collected Poems*, by John Betjeman © The Estate of John Betjeman 1955, 1958, 1962, 1964, 1968, 1970, 1979, 1981, 1982, 2001. Reproduced by permission of John Murray (Publishers); *War Horse* by Nick Stafford, reprinted by permission of Faber and Faber (publishers); 'St Valentine' extract, from *The Wordsworth Dictionary of Saints*, published by Wordsworth Editions (permission sought); *Grace Williams Says It Loud* by Emma Henderson, reproduced by permission of Hodder and Stoughton Limited (publishers) and David Higham Associates; *Life in a Liberty Bodice*, by Christabel Burniston by kind permission of the author; 'Timothy Winters' from *Collected Poems of Charles Causley*, published by Macmillan and reprinted by permission of David Higham Associates; 'London's history' article, reprinted by kind permission of London Tourist (www.londontourist.org); 'Sunken Evening' by Laurie Lee, from *Selected Poems* (1985 Penguin). Reprinted by permission of United Agents on behalf of: The Estate of Laurie Lee; *Rice Without Rain* by Minfong Ho, published by William Morrow an imprint of Harper Collins (permission sought); open letter from Oxfam, reprinted with thanks to Oxfam; *Rising above bullying, from despair to recovery*, Herbert & Hayes (2011), Jessica Kingsley Publishers, London and Philadelphia. Reproduced with permission of Jessica Kingsley Publishers; *Watership Down* by Richard Adams, published by Puffin and reprinted by permission of David Higham Associates; 'Wombat 'the size of a four-wheel drive' found in Australia' article, © Telegraph Media Group Limited 2011; extract from *The Lord God Made Them All* by James Herriot published by Pan Macmillan; 'The Zebras' by Roy Campbell, (permission sought).

Every effort has been made to trace the copyright holders of extracts used in this publication and any outstanding information will be included here at the next available opportunity.

The publishers are grateful to the following for permission to use the photographs and illustrations included in this book:

p. 6 Gijs Bekenkamp/iStockphoto; p. 8 Jupiterimages/Photos.com; p. 15 Luis Pedrosa/Photos.com; p. 22 Ranjan Chari/iStockphoto; p. 25 Mary Evans Picture Library/Alamy; p. 29 Christine Glade/iStockphoto; p. 33 Marcus Lindström/iStockphoto; p. 41 Brandon Bourdages/Stuttershock.com; p. 43 Giorgio Magini/iStockphoto; p. 45 Comstock/Photos.com; p. 51 Photos.com; p. 62 Bikeworldtravel/Shutterstock.com; p. 67 Michael, Arthur C. (fl.1903-28)/Private Collection/The Stapleton Collection/The Bridgeman Art Library; p. 79 Mary Evans Picture Library/Alamy; p. 81 Robyn Mackenzie/Photos.com; p. 84 Clara/Shutterstock.com; p. 87 Photos.com; p. 93 Lisa-Blue/iStockphoto; p. 95 Dutch Photographer, (20th Century)/Private Collection/The Stapleton Collection/The Bridgeman Art Library; p. 99 Catherine Yeulet/Photos.com; p. 102 Stephen_Edwards/Photos.com; p. 109 Anthony Baggett/Photos.com; p. 111 Photos.com; p. 114 S. Greg Panosian/iStockphoto; p. 118 Cagri Oner/iStockphoto; p. 125 Gerri Hernández/iStockPhoto; p. 127 james steidl/Photos.com; p. 131 Chris Schmidt/iStockphoto; p. 136 Byronsdad/iStockphoto; p. 141 Catherine Yeulet/Photos.com; p. 143 William McKelvie/Photos.com; p. 155 NATURAL HISTORY MUSEUM, LONDON/SCIENCE PHOTO LIBRARY; p. 157 Steffen Foerster/Photos.com; p. 162 Jon Schulte/iStockphoto; p. 166 Andre Maritz/Photos.com

Acknowledgements

This book, like its predecessor, *So you really want to learn English Book 1*, is based on everything I've learnt in a long career in English classrooms. And, like all teachers, over the years I've probably learnt as much from my pupils about best practice in English lessons as they have learnt from me. That learning is in this book. So, many thanks go to the hundreds of young people who have passed through my classrooms since 1968.

Sincerest thanks, as always, go to my husband, Nicholas Elkin, who supports me indefatigably as I write these books.

Note to the teacher

This book is intended for use with 11–13 year olds preparing for Common Entrance and other tests and meets the standards set by the National Curriculum at Key Stage 3. Parts of it could also be useful for younger pupils in need of extension work, or for revision or remedial work with an older group.

Each of the ten chapters is based around three themed extracts: one literary prose, one non-fiction and one poem. The oldest extract is Shakespeare in 1609 and the most recent a news report published in 2011. We also wander the world visiting Australia, USA, Thailand and Crete as well as popping down to Antarctica with Coleridge. So there's plenty of variety. Each extract is followed by questions designed to encourage close reading and detailed thinking.

Linked to the extracts is a one-year comprehensive English course taking in poetry technique, personal writing, vocabulary, spelling, grammar, punctuation, speaking and listening and wider reading. Each chapter also includes suggestions for extension tasks under 'And if you've done all that ...'.

New for this edition is a section in each chapter entitled 'Writing workshop' designed to help children to think more carefully about the process of writing in all the different genres required of them.

But don't let's allow testing to become the tail that wags the dog. This book is also about helping children to develop a love of reading. I want them to share the pleasures of rigorous, accurate, effective English – not just to pass examinations, but because I believe that the better you are able to communicate in this lovely language of ours, the more fulfilled you are as a human being.

Susan Elkin

Contents

Chapter 3 Race

Chapter 4 Christmas

Chapter 5 Love

Chapter 6 Growing up

Chapter 7 London

Chapter 8 Drought

Chapter 9 Bullying

Chapter 10 Animals

Introduction

Reading matters

This is a very bookish book. I believe that reading is one of the most essential activities that human beings can undertake. Books do for the mind and soul what food does for the body.

So, almost all the work in this book is based on reading and books. There are questions to encourage you to read closely and carefully. To help you to understand better the tools that poets use in their writing, there is a section on poetry technique in each chapter. Every bit of spelling, vocabulary, grammar and punctuation work is linked to reading. So is much of the speaking and listening. Reading is the backbone of English.

When you are reading a book, it's like a 'direct' phone line between your mind and the author's. You don't need a cast of actors, a TV set, a computer, a teacher, parent or any other assistance. All you need is the printed squiggles on the page and – as if by magic – you are in 'hotline' contact with the mind of, say, Shakespeare (see Chapter 5) who died in 1616 or Dickens (see Chapter 9) who died in 1870. You can share their ideas and stories – instantly. Reading really is remarkable.

That's why every chapter of this book has three separate passages to read and a list of other related reading suggestions under the heading 'Have you read?' I have made these as varied and wide ranging as I can. Don't be discouraged if you find some of these books are difficult to locate – try searching in your local libraries or in second-hand and specialist booksellers including those found online.

Some of the suggestions are quite challenging reads but try not to be put off – part of the joy of reading is to find out about interesting lives and times. Don't tackle hard books in the same way as easier ones. I see the 'Have you read?' sections as a huge buffet offering you lots of delights – many of them probably unfamiliar to you – to taste.

For example, once you've read the jolly passage from Thomas Hardy's 1872 novel *Under the Greenwood Tree* (Chapter 4) you may decide to buy or borrow the book from the library and read the rest of it. Then, if you like it as much as I do, the good news is that Hardy wrote a number of other novels – and they're all out there waiting for you: *Tess of the D'Urbervilles*, *Far from the Madding Crowd* and *The Woodlanders*, for example. He wrote some fine poetry too.

Or perhaps non-fiction is more to your taste. I hope you will learn from, and be entertained by, the passages in this book about St Valentine and growing up in the 1920s. I've also included a speech and a review for variety.

This book also contains ten of my favourite poems (plus a couple of spares in the 'And if you've done all that …' sections). These are poems that I've shared with many classes. I have found that most pupils, most of the time, like most of them as much as I do. So I hope you enjoy them too. Why not make a collection of your own favourites as you browse in anthologies and other books of poems?

You won't, however, confine yourself to the suggestions made in this book. Reading is a personal adventure, a lifelong, unending treasure hunt. Once you get started, every book you finish opens the door to three (at least!) more. You will be thirsting for more by that author, in that style, on that subject, set in that place or about those characters.

If, for example, you enjoy the *Silas Marner* extract in Chapter 5 and then the rest of the novel, you will probably like other novels by George Eliot such as *The Mill on the Floss*. That could lead you to Charlotte Bronte's *Jane Eyre*, which is also about a woman's struggle against 19th century society. Daphne du Maurier's *Rebecca* (1938) is similar to *Jane Eyre* and once you've read that you might like other novels by du Maurier, which might launch you on a quest for more historical fiction (by Philippa Gregory or Rosemary Sutcliff for instance) or novels set in Cornwall … and so on and on. Think of it as a journey and go where it takes you.

Or, if you didn't like a particular book, the opposite will be true. You've discovered something about your reading tastes and will change direction on your journey by looking for something different.

English teachers are always telling their pupils that they need to read more. So what exactly will reading do for you?

The more you read:

- the more you know, because every book has a background, setting and incidental factual information which you soak up through reading a story, usually without realising it;
- the more words you will be familiar with, because keen readers learn new vocabulary every day by seeing words in use and recognising their meaning effortlessly;
- the more interesting things you will have to think about and discuss, because books ask questions and suggest ideas;
- the more ideas you will have for your own writing. Remember, all professional writers read a lot;
- the better you will be able to express yourself in writing and speech, because you will be used to seeing (and hearing in your 'mind's ear') good quality English in a wide range of styles.

Convinced?

Good! Then, let's get started.

Chapter 1 The circus

A visit to the circus

Mark Twain's famous novel *The Adventures of Huckleberry Finn* was first published in America in 1884. It tells, in his own words, the story of the boy Huck who wants to be free. He runs away from his aunt's farm with the adult black slave, Jim. Together they sail northwards up the Mississippi river. On the way, various things happen, such as seeing a circus.

1   It was a real bully circus. It was the splendidest sight that ever was, when they all came riding in, two and two, a gentleman and a lady, side by side, the men just in their drawers and undershorts, and no shoes or stirrups and resting their hands on their thighs, easy and comfortable – there must have
5   been twenty of them – and every lady with a lovely complexion, and perfectly beautiful, and looking like a gang of real sure-enough queens, and dressed in clothes that cost
10   millions of dollars and just littered with diamonds. It was a powerful first sight. I never see anything so lovely. And then one by one they got up
15   and stood and went a-weaving round the ring so gentle and wavy and graceful, the men looking ever so tall and airy and straight with their heads
20   bobbing and skimming along, away up there under the tent roof, and every lady's rose-leafy dress flapping soft and silky round her hips and she
25   looking like the loveliest parasol.

And then faster and faster they went, all of them dancing, first one foot stuck out in the

30 — air and then the other, the horses leaning more and more and the ringmaster going round and round the centre pole, cracking his whip and shouting 'Hi! Hi!' and the clowns cracking jokes behind them. And by and by all hands dropped the reins and every lady put her knuckles on her hips and every gentleman folded his arms and then how the horses did lean over and

35 hump themselves! And so, one after the other they all skipped off into the ring and made the sweetest bow I ever see and then scampered out, and everybody clapped their hands and went just about wild.

Well, all through the circus they done the most astonishing things and all the time that clown carried on so it most killed the people. The ringmaster

40 couldn't ever say a word to him but he was back at him quick as a wink with the funniest things a body ever said – and how he could think of ever so many of them, and so sudden and so pat was what I couldn't noway understand. Why, I couldn't a thought of them in a year. And by and by a drunk man tried to get into the ring – said he wanted to ride. Said he could

45 ride as well as anybody that ever was. They argued and tried to keep him out but he wouldn't listen and the whole show came to a standstill. Then the people began to holler at him and make fun of him and that made him mad and he began to rip and tear. So that stirred up the people and a lot of men begun to pile down off the benches and swarm towards the ring saying,

50 'Knock him down! Throw him out!' and one or two women begun to scream. So then the ringmaster he made a little speech and said he hoped there wouldn't be no disturbance. And if the man would promise he wouldn't make no more trouble he would let him ride if he thought he could stay on the horse. So everybody laughed and said all right and the

55 man got on.

The minute he was on, the horse begun to rip and tear and jump and cavort around with two circus men hanging onto his bridle trying to hold him and the drunk man holding onto his neck and his heels flying in the air at every jump and the whole crowd of people standing up shouting and laughing till

60 the tears rolled down. And at last, sure enough, all the circus men could do, the horse broke loose and away he went like the very nation, round and round the ring with that sot laying down on him and hanging onto his neck with first one leg hanging most to the ground on one side and then t'other one on t'other side and all the people just crazy. It warn't funny to me

65 though, I was all of a tremble to see his danger. But pretty soon he struggled up astraddle and grabbed the bridle, a-reeling his way this and that. And the next minute he dropped the bridle and stood! And the horse going like a

house afire too. He just stood there, a-sailing around as easy and
comfortable as if he warn't ever drunk in his life – and then he begun to
70 pull off his clothes and sling them. He shed them so thick that they kind of
clogged up the air and altogether he shed seventeen suits. And then, there
he was, slim and handsome and dressed the gaudiest and the prettiest you
ever saw and he lit onto that horse with his whip and made him fairly hum.
And finally skipped off and made his bow and danced off to the dressing
75 room and everybody just a-howling with pleasure and astonishment.

Then the ringmaster he see how he had been fooled and he was the sickest
ringmaster you ever see, I reckon. Why, it was one of his own men! He had
got up that joke all out of his own head and never let on to anybody. Well, I
felt sheepish enough to be took in so, but I wouldn't a been in that
80 ringmaster's place, not for a thousand dollars.

From *The Adventures of Huckleberry Finn* by Mark Twain (1884)

EXERCISE 1.1

Now answer these questions as fully as you can. Quote from the passage in your
answers:

1. Provide a word or phrase of your own which means the same as the
    following words as they are used in this passage: (a) bully (line 1), (b) holler
    (line 47), (c) cavort (line 56), (d) astraddle (line 66), (e) lit (line 73),
    (f) sheepish (line 79).

2. How would you know from the passage that this story is set in America
    even if you had not been told?

3. Explain in your own words Huck's initial reaction to the circus.

4. How does Huck feel when he realises the truth about the 'drunk man'?

5. What impression do you get of Huck's character from this passage?

6. What is unusual about Huck's language and why do think Twain makes him
    speak in this way?

Retirement for Britain's last performing elephant

Here a journalist, writing for a popular tabloid Sunday newspaper, reports on the final freeing of a long-abused circus elephant.

1   Abused circus elephant Anne took her first steps towards freedom this weekend after years of misery.

In a victory for *Sunday Mirror* readers, who backed our six-year campaign with Born Free for her release, Britain's last circus elephant is to move to
5   Longleat Safari Park.

Once an elephant house is refurbished, 59-year-old Anne, in constant pain from chronic arthritis, will set off on her 150-mile journey.

The move comes just days after a video of her being
10   hit with a pitchfork was released by animal welfare group Animal Defenders International.

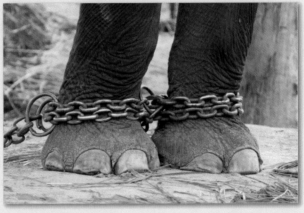

Her release was greeted
15   with delight by Robert Sheret, 56, who repeatedly tried to stop Anne being abused while he worked at Bobby Roberts Super Circus from 1983 to 85.

20   He said: "When I complained she and the other elephants were being beaten, and weren't getting enough exercise or food, Bobby Roberts told me: 'I pay you to work, not to think. They're my elephants and I can do what I like.'

"After two years I couldn't take any more and I left."

25   This week Bobby and wife Moira claimed they'd been trying to find a retirement home for Anne for two years, surprising campaigners whose offers to re-home her have been refused.

Robert said: "The only reason he's letting her go now is because she's too sick to go on the road any more and earn her keep."

30   He spoke out as the RSPCA took charge of Anne on Friday.

Even before the video film scandal broke, Bobby chose to leave Anne at her winter quarters in Polebrook, Northants, when the circus began its annual tour two weeks ago.

From an article by Susie Boniface published in the *Sunday Mirror* (April 2011)

EXERCISE 1.2

Answer the following questions:

1. Which three charities have been involved in securing Anne's release?

2. Who owned Anne during her circus career?

3. Where is Anne now going to live?

4. Give another word or phrase for (a) refurbished (line 6), (b) chronic (line 7).

5. Who is Robert Sheret?

6. What do you learn about Anne's previous owners from this passage?

'Circus Lion'

1   Lumbering haunches, pussyfoot tread, a pride of
Lions under the arcs
Walk in, leap up, sit pedestalled there and glum
As a row of Dickensian clerks.

5   Their eyes are slag[1]. Only a muscle flickering
A bored theatrical roar
Witness now to the furnaces that drove them
Exultant along the spoor[2].

In preyward, elastic leap they are sent through paper
10   Hoops at another's will
And a whip's crack: afterwards in their cages
They tear the provided kill.

Caught young, can this public animal ever dream of
Stars, distances and thunders?
15   Does he twitch in sleep for ticks, dried water-holes,
Rogue elephants or hunters?

Sawdust, not burning desert, is the ground
Of his to-fro, to-fro pacing,
Barred with the zebra stripes that imply
20   Sun's free wheel, man's coercing.

See this abdicated beast, once king
Of them all, nibble his claws:
Not anger enough left – no, nor despair –
To break his teeth on the bars.

Cecil Day Lewis (1962)

Notes:
[1] Coal waste left in heaps near mines. Dull, dark grey in colour.
[2] Scented trail left by an animal

Poetry technique: rhythm

Rhythm is the pattern made by an arrangement of short and long sounds. It can be regular and even or irregular and unpredictable. Think of the sound patterns made by a percussion instrument such as a drum in an orchestra or band. Words work like percussion instruments too and all language has rhythm.

When, for instance, we say 'Lumbering' and 'pussyfoot' we stress the first syllable and follow it with two quick syllables. It sounds like the pattern of the lion's feet – first the heavier front ones, followed by the lighter back legs.

Look for other interesting examples of rhythm in 'Circus Lion' and in the poems used in other chapters of this book.

EXERCISE 1.3

Now answer these questions. Quote the words of the poem in your answers:

1. Describe in your own words how the lions behave when they first appear.

2. What is the significance of (a) zebra stripes (line 19), (b) abdicated (line 21).

3. Why is 'to-fro, to-fro pacing' (line 18) effective?

4. Choose and comment on three words or phrases which you find interesting and effective.

5. What do the unanswered questions in the fourth verse tell you about the poet's attitude to performing animals?

6. How, by the end of the poem, does the poet imagine that the lions are feeling?

Your turn to write

EXERCISE 1.4

1. Write about a circus or some other sort of live show, play or performance that you have seen.

2. What are your views about performing animals in TV programmes and advertisements and other sorts of production – as well as in circuses?

3. Write a story entitled either 'Circus' or 'Lions'.

4. Imagine you are Anne the elephant and write your story.

5. Write about a circus in any way you wish.

6. Write about a new experience.

Writing workshop

Starting a story

If you have a story you want to write with all the main ideas in your head, you have to decide where, when and with whom to begin – and that can be quite tricky.

Take the story of The Three Bears, for instance. Goldilocks presumably leaves home for her early morning walk at about the same time as the bears go out leaving their porridge to cool. So, do you start with Goldilocks or the bears? Whichever you choose you will have to double back and explain the other. You cannot tell it in the exact order that things happened.

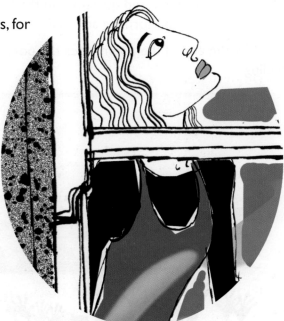

There are also other ways you could start to tell the story.

EXERCISE 1.5

You could do this exercise in writing or in a pair as an oral exercise taking it in turns to tell each other the different versions.

Remember that, although this is a well-known traditional story, you as story teller are free to invent your own details to attach to the framework of the original story.

Modernise it if you like. Say what the characters were wearing and what they did when they weren't making, eating or stealing porridge – if you wish:

1. Tell The Three Bears story starting with the bears.

2. Tell The Three Bears story starting with Goldilocks.

3. Tell The Three Bears story starting with the drama of the bears finding Goldilocks asleep and then fill in the details of what has happened to lead up to this.

4. Tell The Three Bears story as if you were Baby Bear. Think about where you will start.

5. Tell The Three Bears story in a different way and with a different starting point from 1, 2, 3 and 4.

Discuss with a partner which of these versions you think works best and why.

Grammar and punctuation

There are eight main **parts of speech** or word classes:

noun	**verb**	**adjective**	**adverb**
pronoun	**conjunction**	**preposition**	**article**

Almost every word in any context belongs to one of these eight word classes, most of which will already be familiar to you.

This chapter and the next revise the first four; pronouns and conjunctions are covered in Chapter 3 and prepositions and articles in Chapter 4.

Nouns
Nouns are naming words. They can be singular or plural. The class includes **proper nouns** (e.g. 'Huck', 'Manchester'), **abstract nouns** (e.g. 'pleasure', 'astonishment') and **collective nouns** (e.g. 'pride' – of lions, 'pack' – of cards).

EXERCISE 1.6

Write these sentences and underline the nouns:

1.   Mark Twain was American.

2.   Lions, tigers and panthers are big cats.

3.   As the Land Rover moved forward with caution, we saw a single elephant and then a whole herd.

4.   The circus is coming to town.

5.   Anne waved her trunk and then, to our joy, she trumpeted.

6.   Hunger was gnawing at me, so I ate some biscuits.

Verbs

Verbs are action or doing words. A verb can consist of several words such as 'will have been eating' or 'is running'. The words 'will have been' and 'is' are auxiliary words. These **auxiliary** words are generally there to show the **tense** of the verb, i.e. **when** the action is happening (past, present or future).

EXERCISE 1.7

Put verbs of your own in the following sentences. Make some of them consist of more than one word:

1.   They _____ the public to boycott the circus.

2.   All the pupils in this class _____.

3.   Afterwards in their cages they _____ the provided kill.

4.   I _____ and you _____.

5.   Please don't _____.

6.   He _____ the bridle and _____.

Adjectives

Adjectives qualify or **modify** nouns. That means that they change the meaning of the noun or tell you more about it. 'He was a quiet man' means something quite different from 'He was a man'.

Mark Twain makes Huck use a lot of adjectives. Reread the passage at the beginning of this chapter. Count the adjectives in the first paragraph and work out why you think there are so many.

Remember that you can never assign words to their word classes unless they are in a context – usually a sentence. This is because words can, and often do, change class according to the job they're doing. It's a bit like your being in one school group, class or set for Maths, but another for French.

For example, consider the words 'break' and 'set':

Try not to **break** that valuable vase. (verb)

I really enjoy **break** buns. (adjective)

Break is my favourite part of the morning. (noun)

The gamekeeper **set** the trap to catch a rabbit. (verb)

The tennis match had reached **set** point. (adjective)

Freddy is in the top **set** for science. (noun)

EXERCISE 1.8

Use each of these words in several different sentences of your own so that they belong to different word classes for each use:

part   mean   lift   fast   strip   flower

EXERCISE 1.9

As you know, every sentence needs to begin with a capital letter and to end with a full stop, question mark or exclamation mark. Punctuate the following sentences correctly:

1. what a book

2. one of my favourite authors is Mark Twain

3. have you read all Cecil Day Lewis's poems

4. shall I pour the tea

5. no I won't

6. it is quite easy to punctuate accurately

Spell check: -ful words

Although the word 'full' has a double 'l', the related suffix '-ful' in adjectives such as 'beautiful', 'wonderful' and 'powerful' and in nouns such as 'cupful', 'spoonful', 'handful' and 'armful' has only one.

EXERCISE 1.10

Make a list of as many words ending in '-ful' as you can think of. Arrange them in two columns, one for adjectives and one for nouns.

To form an adverb from adjectives ending in '-ful', add 'ly'. That gives a double 'l'. So:

forget**ful**	forget**fully**
youth**ful**	youth**fully**
use**ful**	use**fully**

Think carefully when you form a plural from a '-ful' noun. It is the main part of the word which takes the 's', not the suffix. So:

one spadeful	three spadesful
one hatful	six hatsful
one teaspoonful	two teaspoonsful

EXERCISE 1.11

Learn carefully the spellings of these ten words, all of which are taken from the two passages and the poem at the beginning of this chapter:

stirrup	complexion	loveliest	handsome	rogue
campaigners	campaign	released	arthritis	annual

Vocabulary

Eponyms

The word 'Dickensian' is an eponym – a name which became a word. Behind every eponym there's a story.

Charles Dickens (1812–1870) was an English novelist, author of *Oliver Twist* and *David Copperfield*. The adjective 'Dickensian' describes almost anything Victorian which Dickens features in one of his many books.

EXERCISE 1.12

Match the following ten people's names to the sentences about them:

Charles Macintosh, Dr Rudolph Diesel, Lord Sandwich, Louis Pasteur, Louis Braille, the Duke of Wellington, Alessandro Volta, Monsieur Nicot, Laszlo Biro, Adolphe Sax.

1. He devised a new method of sterilising milk.

2. He invented a new musical instrument.

3. He first introduced tobacco to France.

4. He was a great gambler and, to avoid leaving the gambling tables for a meal, he asked for a slice of meat between two slices of bread.

5. He invented a new type of engine oil, in which ignition of fuel is produced by the heat of air suddenly compressed.

6. He invented the electric battery and gave his name to a unit of electromotive force.

7. He wore knee-length rubber boots during military campaigns.

8. He patented a coat made of waterproof material.

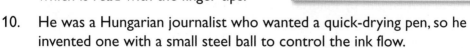

9. Blinded by a childhood accident, he invented a language of raised dots which is read with the finger tips.

10. He was a Hungarian journalist who wanted a quick-drying pen, so he invented one with a small steel ball to control the ink flow.

EXERCISE 1.13

Use a good dictionary or the internet to find out and write notes on the origins of these eponyms:

1. hoover
2. morse
3. lynch
4. mesmerise
5. guillotine
6. bloomers
7. cardigan
8. silhouette
9. jacuzzi
10. watt

Speaking and listening

1. Work with a partner or in a small group. Practise reading the extract from *The Adventures of Huckleberry Finn* aloud. You will probably find yourselves slipping into a southern American accent – even if you don't try to – because that's the way Twain makes Huck speak.

2. Learn the poem 'Circus Lion' by heart and practise reciting it. Perform it for the rest of the class or to a smaller group.

3. Prepare a short talk either in favour of performing animals in circuses or against it. There is plenty of information about this on the internet. Type 'performing animals' into Google or another search engine.

4. Read one of the books listed in 'Have you read?' (below). Tell the class about it.

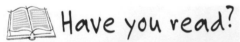 Have you read?

All of these are stories about circuses, elephants or the southern USA. I have also included a book with more poems by C Day Lewis. (The dates given show when these books were first published.)

- *The Adventures of Huckleberry Finn* by Mark Twain (1884)
- *The Adventures of Tom Sawyer* by Mark Twain (1876)
- *The Road to Memphis* by Mildred E Taylor (1990)
- *The Land* by Mildred E Taylor (2003)
- *Dodgem* by Bernard Ashley (1981)
- *Uncle Tom's Cabin* by Harriet Beecher Stowe (1852)

- *Elephant Bill* by J H H Williams (1956)
- *The Complete Poems of C Day Lewis* edited by Jill Balcon (1992)
- *Olivia's First Term* by Lyn Gardner (2011)
- *Circus Shoes* by Noel Streatfeild (1956, first published as *The Circus is Coming* in 1938)

✔ And if you've done all that ...

- Several states in America have banned the use of *The Adventures of Huckleberry Finn* in schools on the grounds that it is a racist novel. This is mostly because Huck consistently refers to his friend Jim as a 'nigger'. Read the novel very carefully and decide what you think. Work out the reasons for your opinion. *The Day They Came to Arrest the Book* by Nat Hentoff (1985) might help with this. It's a novel about a school from which Huckleberry Finn is banned.

- Consider the whole subject of banning books. Is it ever right? If so, for what reasons and who should decide? Read *Fahrenheit 451* by Ray Bradbury (1953) – the title refers to the temperature at which books burn.

  www.theweewebb.co.uk/banned_books.php lists titles which have been banned somewhere in America. You could use your research as the basis for an article in the school magazine. You might also organise a class or school debate on the subject.

- Read Chapter 3 of *Hard Times* (1854) by Charles Dickens. In it, Mr Gradgrind is horrified to find two of his children watching, and enjoying, a circus act. You might then want to read the rest of the novel.

Chapter 2 Survival

Stranded

The following is an essay which critically analyses a passage in William Golding's famous 1954 novel, *Lord of the Flies*. It tells the story of a group of privileged schoolboys stranded on a tropical island after a plane crash. In the passage, which comes from the end of Chapter 1, some of them are exploring the island.

This piece of writing is included as an extended example of how you, yourself, might write analytical essays about passages you have studied.

1   The story is told in the third person as if there were an invisible observer –
       the omniscient or all-knowing author – describing what the characters say,
       do, see, hear, think and experience. It is a device which allows Golding to be
       unobtrusively inside the minds of his characters.

5   He knows, for example, that the boys have previously guessed that they are
       on an island, that they feel triumphant, that they are savouring 'the right of
       domination' and that they understand 'what an enormity the downstroke
       would be' when Jack hesitates over the trapped piglet.

       This common story telling technique enables Golding to tell his story in
10   adult language. Had he chosen to make one of his characters a narrator he
       would have been obliged to use the sort of language which the boys
       themselves use – which might have limited him.

       Thus, the adult narrator observes that 'The bushes were dark evergreen
       and aromatic and the many buds were waxen green and folded up against
15   the light' which is a very detailed observation in comparison with Jack's
       terse comment 'Candle buds.' It is as if the adult narrator is providing a
       commentary behind the boys' dialogue.

       Because this passage comes from near the beginning of the novel Golding
       has to paint a vivid picture of the island which is meant to seem, when the
20   boys first arrive there, like an unspoiled paradise. He wants the reader to
       compare it with, for example, the Garden of Eden in the Bible (Genesis
       chapters 2 and 3) before everything goes wrong.

       He describes colour – 'the pink rocks,' 'the peacock blue' of the lagoon and
       the 'dark blue of the sea.' Other sensations include the breeze which 'blew
25   cool on their faces,' the scents of the vegetation, awareness of plants under

their feet and the frenzied screams of the trapped piglet. It is very sensuous writing.

Golding's description of the long, thin island is precise and accurate. Placing the boys on the top of a mountain with a bird's eye view of the whole
30 island means that the author can present the island exactly as they see it – boat shaped with the angled coral reef along part of two sides, the offshore rock at the other end and so on. From the information provided in this passage you could draw a reasonably accurate map and sketch the terrain.

Colourful imagery adds to the intensity of the description. The coral reef
35 looks like a giant's scribble. The navicular image for the island is appropriate because it is on the sea. Comparing the lagoon with an aquarium refers to the fish which inhabit it as well as to the colour and clarity of the water. The site of the air crash resembles a wound on the island: 'a visible gash' and a 'scar.'

40 As a way of emphasising the luxuriance of the island and the intensity of the boys' feelings, Golding uses a number of lists. The butterflies, for instance are 'lifting, fluttering, settling.' On either side of the mountain are 'rocks, cliffs, treetops and a steep slope'. The voice of the piglet is 'thin, needle-sharp and insistent'. The boys 'laughed and tumbled and shouted'.

45 Most of these lists consist of three items – a traditional way of making something seem elegant, rounded and powerful in a story. Folk stories often tell of three people, three events, three wishes and so on. In the Bible, three gifts were brought to the infant Jesus (Matthew Chapter 2) and Christians worship a God in three parts – the Holy Trinity. In the passage only three
50 boys – Simon, Jack and Ralph – have gone to the top of the mountain to survey the island although they can see many others: 'insect-like figures' down by the beach.

Golding begins to develop the characters of the three boys in this passage by showing us what
55 they do and say – or don't say. All the dialogue is very brief. We learn quite a lot about the boys from what they don't say. They are actively thinking and feeling as Golding makes clear.

60 Ralph's simple comment 'This belongs to us' has dignity and maturity. Later he 'wisely' notices evidence that the island is uninhabited and that the 'candle buds' are just

buds on a bush. He also makes dramatic gestures with his hands and arms and instigates the descent from the mountain. He is already showing the

65   signs of responsible, thoughtful leadership.

Simon, on the other hand, is a dreamer. He is quieter, at one point looking silently at the others with his face 'glowing'. And it is Simon who first notices that the buds on the bush are like candles and marvels at it: 'Like candles. Candle bushes. Candle buds.'

70 Jack, in contrast, shows raw excitement and impetuosity. He likes the idea of

75 hunting and catching things – fending for himself until adults arrive to

80 take command of life again. He is dismissive of Simon's suggestion that

85 the buds resemble candles because they are not a source of food. The

90 destructiveness he shows in hacking pointlessly at the buds points to an

95 aggressive streak too, although he cannot bring himself to kill the piglet.

100 There is a film-

like quality to Golding's writing here. First the boys hear the pig and charge forward – and exhilarated Jack raises the knife 'with a flourish'. Then there's a pause as if the action has gone into slow motion. The pig goes on screaming and struggling while the knife glitters and Jack hesitates. When
105 the animal breaks free it is almost as though the boys, completely disconcerted in 'the place of terror' are relieved, although they are ashamed of feeling as they do and don't admit it to each other.

Susan Elkin (2012)

EXERCISE 2.1

Now find a copy of the novel *Lord of the Flies* (from your teacher or your library), read the passage (starts with "They were on the tip of a cirque" and ends with "and began to climb back to the track") the essay above discusses, and answer these questions:

1. Explain the meaning of (a) lavishly, (b) petered, (c) bastion, (d) savoured, (e) aromatic, (f) hiatus.

2. Why do the boys climb to a high point?

3 What is the boys' most urgent practical problem?

4. Which of the boys seems to be emerging as the leader? Give reasons for your answer.

5. What do you learn about Jack's personality from this passage?

6. Summarise the nature of the island and its wildlife. Use your own words.

7. Why do the boys feel ashamed at the end of the passage?

A dramatisation of *Lord of the Flies* in Regent's Park

In summer 2011 *Lord of the Flies* was presented as an open air play in London. This is a review of the show from *The Stage*, a weekly newspaper read mostly by people who work in the entertainments industries and those who would like to.

1   William Golding's 1954 post-war parable about the fragility of civilisation wears well and makes strong physical theatre – an arresting debut for the Open Air Theatre's 2011 season. This adaptation, incidentally, provides more exciting roles for young men than anything since *The History Boys*.

5   The evocative set (by Jon Bausor) is strewn with the debris of travel – suitcases, water bottles, children's toys, life vests, clothing – around the half buried fuselage of the crashed plane from which the boys have escaped. It is not pretty and

10 cleverly reflects the chaos the boys work through on the island.

Although the ensemble work is strong, the show belongs to George Bukhari as Piggy, the

15 troubled but clear-sighted boy (despite his myopia, which is part of the plot) who is of the 'wrong' social class and wants rules, order and democracy, while

20 most of the others favour the excitement of savagery. Bukhari is a very sensitive actor. James Clay gives a fine performance as the power-hungry Jack and

25 Alistair Toovey's Ralph is thoughtful and appropriately dignified.

The war-painted boys dance and whoop as they kill the pig and hunt the elusive beast – a symbol of superstition and religion – and terrorise Simon (immaculate work by Joshua Williams) and Piggy. Once the point is made,

30 however, it does not need several repeats and the whole show is half an hour too long.

Lord of the Flies is an alarmingly truthful and therefore deeply disturbing account of human nature and, if overheard audience comments on press night were anything to go by, this new, highly visual version will introduce it
35 to many people to whom it is unfamiliar.

Production information

By:	William Golding, adapted by Nigel Williams
Composer:	Nick Powell
Management:	Regent's Park Open Air Theatre
40 **Cast:**	George Bukhari, James Clay, Sam Clemmett, Theo Cowan, Matt Ingram, Jordan Maxwell, James McConville, Stuart Matthews, Alistair Toovey, Joshua Williams, Harrison Sansostri, Spike White, Adam Thomas Wright
Director:	Timothy Sheader and Liam Steel
45 **Design:**	Jon Bausor
Sound:	Mike Walker
Lighting:	James Farncombe

From an article by Susan Elkin published in *The Stage* (June 2011)

EXERCISE 2.2

Now answer these questions:

1. Who (a) played Piggy, (b) adapted the novel, (c) designed the set, (d) was responsible for lighting?

2. Where was this play staged?

3. Give another word or phrase for (a) parable (line 1), (b) evocative (line 5), (c) fuselage (line 7), (d) elusive (line 28).

4. Describe the set for this play in your own words.

5. What do you learn about the character of Piggy from this review?

6. List three adjectives which show that, on the whole, the reviewer enjoyed this play.

7. What did the reviewer *not* like about this production?

8. What did the reviewer notice about other audience members?

'Death of an Aircraft'

An incident of the Cretan campaign 1941
To George Psychoundakis

1   One day on our village in the month of July
        An aeroplane sank from the sea of the sky,
                White as a whale it smashed on the shore
                Bleeding oil and petrol all over the floor.

5   The Germans advanced in the vertical heat
        To save the dead plane from the people of Crete,
                And round the glass wreck in a circus of snow
                Set seven mechanical sentries to go.

        Seven stalking spiders about the sharp sun
10   Clicking like clockwork and each with a gun
                But at 'Come to the Cookhouse' they wheeled about
                And sat down to sausages and sauerkraut.

        Down from the mountain burning so brown
        Wriggled three heroes from Kastelo town,
15   Deep in the sand they silently sank
                And each struck a match for the petrol tank.

        Up went the plane in a feather of fire
        As the bubbling boys began to retire
                And, grey in the guardhouse, seven Berliners
20   Lost their stripes as well as their dinners.

        Down in the village, at murder-stations,
        The Germans fell in friends and relations:
                But not a Kastelian snapped an eye
                As he spat in the air and prepared to die.

25   Not a Kastelian whispered a word
        Dressed with the dust to be massacred,
                And squinted up at the sky with a frown
                As three bubbly boys came walking down.

        One was sent to the county gaol
30   Too young for bullets if not for bail,
                But the other two were in prime condition
                To take on a load of ammunition.

In Archontiki they stood in the weather
Naked, hungry, chained together:
      Stark as the stones in the market place,
      Under the eyes of the populace.

Their irons unlocked as their naked hearts
They faced the squad and their funeral carts.
      The Captain cried, 'Before you're away
      Is there any last word you'd like to say?'

'I want no words,' said one 'with my lead,
Only some water to cool my head.'
      'Water,' the other said, 'is all very fine
      But I'll be taking a glass of wine.

A glass of wine for the afternoon
With permission to sing a signature tune'.
      And he ran the raki down his throat
      And took a deep breath for the leading note.

But before the squad could shoot or say
Like the impala he leapt away
      Over the rifles, under the biers,
      The bullets rattling round his ears.

35

40

45

50

'Run!' they cried to the boy of stone
Who now stood there in the street alone,
55   But, 'Rather than bring revenge on your head
It is better for me to die,' he said.

The soldiers turned their machine-guns round
And shot him down with a dreadful sound
        Scrubbed his face with perpetual dark
60   And rubbed it out like a pencil mark.

But his comrade slept in the olive tree
And sailed by night on the gnawing sea,
        The soldier's silver shilling earned
        And, armed like an archangel, returned.

Charles Causley

Poetry technique: metaphor and simile

Poets (and other writers) continually describe things by comparing them with other things.

Charles Causley's aircraft is 'white as a whale'. This is an example of a **simile**. A simile is a comparison in which the writer uses 'as' or 'like' to indicate what he or she is comparing the item to. Examples are 'like a pencil mark' in 'Death of an Aircraft' and 'glum as a row of Dickensian clerks' in 'Circus Lion' in Chapter 1.

In 'Death of an Aircraft' Causley refers to the German guards as 'seven stalking spiders'. This is a shorter, neater sort of comparison and is known as a **metaphor**. He writes as if the guards actually are spiders and expects you to understand what he means.

Sometimes a metaphor can be a single word. Look at 'barred' in 'Circus Lion'.

Make a list of similes and metaphors in 'Death of an Aircraft' and 'Circus Lion'. Work out what each one means and what it adds to the poem.

Together similes and metaphors are known as **imagery** because they create pictures (as in the French word *images*) and work on your imagination.

EXERCISE 2.3

Read 'Death of an Aircraft'. Now answer these questions as fully as you can. Try to quote the words of the poem in your responses:

1. Summarise in your own words the story which the poem is telling. Use no more than five sentences.

2. What comparison does the poet use in the first verse to create a picture of the aircraft and its surroundings? How effective do you find it?

3. Explain the meaning of (a) squinted (line 27), (b) signature tune (line 46), (c) perpetual (line 59), (d) gnawing (line 62).

4. 'Too young for bullets if not for bail / But the other two were in prime condition / To take on a load of ammunition.' What is the poet really saying here?

5. Do you think the poem ends in a positive or negative way? Give reasons for your view.

6. What does the rhyme scheme add to the poem?

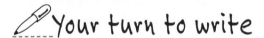 Your turn to write

EXERCISE 2.4

1. Imagine you are one of the boys in *Lord of the Flies* who was later rescued. Tell the story of your time on the island. Add as much detail as you like.

2. Write a poem about someone surviving under unlikely circumstances. If you wish, you can copy Charles Causley's four-line verse pattern or organise your poem in any other way you like.

3. Imagine a dramatic shipwreck or airwreck. Write a newspaper report of it.

4. Write your own desert island story.

5. Why do you think so many stories have been made up and/or told about survival and rescue? Write your views.

6. Write about survival in any way you wish.

 Writing workshop

Writing a review

A review is an account of something which the writer has experienced and wants to tell others about. It could relate, for example to:

- a film, TV programme, play or music performance the reviewer has seen
- a book the reviewer has read
- a restaurant the reviewer has eaten at
- a hotel the reviewer has stayed in
- art or some other exhibition or show the reviewer has seen.

A review has two main purposes:

- It tells the reader, who may never do whatever it is the reviewer has done, enough about it to feel that he or she has shared the experience.
- It helps the reader to decide whether or not to read the book, see the film, eat at the restaurant, visit the exhibition or not.

Some points to help you write your own reviews:

- Include some description of the experience. If it's a book give a brief account of the plot (without revealing anything which would spoil it for another reader). If it's a restaurant, describe the room and table settings and say what you ate.
- Everything you write should be specific. Don't write: My lasagne was horrible. Write: My lasagne was tasteless and undercooked and needed a lot more cheese. Don't write: This book was really good and I recommend it to anyone my age. Write: This book, which I can't recommend too highly, gripped me from beginning to end largely because the plot is so strong that you can't wait to see what happens next.
- Be very careful with your adjectives. If you use too many – or rely on meaningless ones such as 'exciting' and 'amazing' – your review will sound overwritten and false.
- Remember to praise (or criticise) the creators of the experience – the author, film director, chef or hotel owner.
- If your review relates to any sort of performing arts experience (like the review of *Lord of the Flies* in this chapter) you will also need to mention some of the performers and backstage professionals.
- If you are writing about a book mention things like characterisation, plot and ideas.
- If you know you are going to review something it makes sense to jot down your thoughts at the time so that you have some notes to work from.

EXERCISE 2.5

Write a review of a book you have recently read, a show you have seen, an event you have attended, a restaurant meal you have eaten, somewhere you have stayed, or any other 'reviewable' experience you have had.

Keep your review short – maximum 250 words – and follow the guidelines above.

Grammar and punctuation

Adjectives

An **adjective** qualifies or modifies a noun. It adds to its meaning or tells you more about it:

> **cupping** gesture
>
> **many** buds
>
> **deep** breath
>
> **dreadful** sound
>
> **helicopter** pilot

The adjective doesn't necessarily go next to the noun it qualifies:

> The rescue man was **great**.
>
> They stood in the weather / **Naked**, **hungry**.
>
> Its voice was **thin**, **needle-sharp**, **insistent**.

EXERCISE 2.6

Write the following sentences. Underline the adjectives. Draw a line linking them to the nouns they qualify:

1. Ralph sketched a twining line from the bald spot.

2. Simon's face was red.

3. And, grey in the guardhouse, seven Berliners / Lost their stripes as well as their dinners.

4. The production of *Lord of the Flies* in Regent's Park was thrilling.

5. Well-respected and admired, Charles Causley was a fine poet.

6. They ran, thin and eager, along the shore.

Adverbs

Adverbs qualify or modify verbs:

They **silently** sank.

All three laughed **ashamedly**.

She **often** said.

She **hardly** cried.

Or sometimes they modify other adverbs or adjectives:

very quickly

happily married

They tell you **how** or **when** something is done or happens.

Occasionally an adverb modifies a whole sentence:

Unfortunately, it's raining today.

We learnt, **however**, that games had been cancelled.

EXERCISE 2.7

Write the following sentences underlining the adverbs:

1. Sadly, there will not be time to visit this museum.

2. We said we were extremely sorry and left.

3 Are you still hungry?

4. We need to get this work done fast.

5. Dismally and reluctantly, they packed up their tent.

6. Jabinda moved forwards while Fred slid backwards, but both should have been going clockwise.

Commas

Remember that a sentence begins with a **capital letter** and ends with a **full stop, exclamation** or **question mark**. Think of it as a closed box.

Inside the box you may – or may not – need **commas** for various reasons.

For example, commas can be used to separate the name of the person being spoken to from the rest of the sentence:

'Oliver, please put the chairs straight.'

'What do you think, Emma?'

'Did you know, Mum, that I had made the supper?'

Or you can use them to divide the items in a list – which can be nouns, adjectives, adverbs or verbs – but not before the final 'and':

I bought oranges, bananas, apples, peaches and plums.

The children ran, skipped, hopped, jumped and thoroughly enjoyed themselves.

My father came in with a delightful, tiny, wriggling brown puppy.

We did it happily, willingly, knowingly and fast.

EXERCISE 2.8

Discuss with a partner where the commas should go in the following examples. Be sure that you know exactly why you need a comma where you do:

1. 'Peter please bring me the paper glue stapler and pens.'

2. 'Did you see that enormous slinky black cat?'

3. 'What an amazing story Jake!'

4. We heard Perry playing singing and tuning his violin while his twin sister Abigail was outside trampolining catching throwing and exercising.

5. 'Everybody will you listen please!'

6. Maria's Tuesday lessons included Maths PE Geography English and French.

7. 'Sit down Melissa and I'll explain.'

Spell check: suffixes

Words ending in '-e' usually drop the 'e' when 'y' or **suffixes** beginning with a vowel such as 'ed', 'er' or 'ing' are added. So:

stone	stony
enquire	enquiry
combine	combination
suppose	supposing
declare	declaration
spice	spicy

But words ending in '-e' to which a suffix beginning with a consonant is added retain their 'e'. So:

advance	advancement
face	faceless
blame	blameworthy
fire	fireproof
house	household

'Awful' (awe) and 'argument' (argue) are exceptions. Learn them.

EXERCISE 2.9

Add as many suffixes as you can think of to form different, correctly spelt words to the following base words:

1. mouse
2. lace
3. noise
4. bite
5. require
6. price
7. shoe
8. free
9. service
10. peace

EXERCISE 2.10

Check that you can spell these ten words from the passages in this chapter:

| guessed | descent | parallel | aquarium | flourish |
| aeroplane | mechanical | wriggled | massacred | debris |

Vocabulary

Circum- words

William Golding uses the geographical term 'cirque' for a feature which is called a 'cwm' in Wales and a 'corrie' in Scotland.

Cirque is a French word which came originally from the Latin word for 'ring': *circus*. We get 'circle', 'circular', 'circuit' and many other words from the same root. A circus was traditionally a performance in a ring and at Piccadilly Circus, for example, the traffic makes a ring round a central point (the statue of Eros, in the case of Piccadilly Circus).

The Latin word *circum*, which stems from *circus*, is also used as a prefix. It means 'around' and various English words derive from it.

EXERCISE 2.11

Put the correct words beginning with circum- into these sentences. The words you need are listed at the end:

1. One of the boys in Charles Causley's poem managed to _____ the German occupation.

2. When we practise speaking and listening, we are always advised to avoid _____ and to be very direct.

3. The outer edge of any circle is known as the _____.

4. I like to read the _____ on my grandfather's medals.

5. My elder brother keeps his thoughts well reined in but my younger brother is much less _____.

circumscription   circumvent   circumference   circumspect   circumlocution

---

Toponyms

A 'Berliner' is someone who lives in Berlin. A 'Venetian' is an inhabitant of Venice.

Words like 'Berliner' and 'Venetian' are **toponyms**, from the Greek *topos*, meaning 'place'.

EXERCISE 2.12

Where do people with the following toponyms come from?

1. Mancunian   6. Sicilian

2. Parisian   7. Oxonian

3. Londoner   8. Hamburger

4. Neopolitan   9. Glaswegian

5. Liverpudlian   10. Florentine

EXERCISE 2.13

You were advised earlier in this chapter about the dangers of 'overwriting', in particular when writing reviews. Use the following over- words in sentences of your own to show that you understand their meaning:

1.	overreact	6.	overdraw
2.	overburden	7.	overlap
3.	overdress	8.	overhear
4.	overfamiliar	9.	overcome
5.	overcast	10.	overlook

Speaking and listening

1. Interview someone who has survived something. Many older people remember the bombing of London and other cities in the 1940s, for example. Or you may know someone who has survived a serious accident or illness. Ask them who, what, when, why and how questions.

2. Work with a partner. Imagine that one of you is in a very dangerous situation and the other is the rescuer. Work out the exact circumstances and what you would say to each other.

3. Work in a group of five or six. Choose a role each – probably someone famous or important. Imagine you are in a hot air balloon which is losing height. The only way the balloon will stay in the air is if weight is shed and that means one of the occupants must be thrown out. Take turns to persuade the group that you – in your role – should not be the one. Once you've had a bit of practice at this, you and your teacher might be able to organise a whole class balloon debate.

4. Prepare a short talk called 'How to Survive'. Interpret this in any way you like (it need not be serious). Give your talk to the rest of the class.

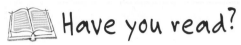 # Have you read?

All of these are stories about survival at various points in history and the future:

- *Lord of the Flies* by William Golding (1954)
- *Robinson Crusoe* by Daniel Defoe (1719)
- *Parcel of Patterns* by Jill Paton Walsh (1983)
- *Plague 99* by Jean Ure (1989)
- *Death of Grass* by John Christopher (1956)
- *Z for Zachariah* by Robert O'Brien (1975)
- *Kensuke's Kingdom* by Michael Morpurgo (1999)
- *Brother in the Land* by Robert Swindells (1984)
- *Wreckers* by Julie Hearn (2011)
- *Walkabout* by James Vance Marshall (1959)
- *The Odyssey* by Homer (c. eighth century BC)

✔ And if you've done all that ...

- Read Shakespeare's play *The Tempest* (you might want to see it as a staged play or on film first), really an early example of a shipwreck survival story. Try also to see a production or watch a video of the play. Make an informative poster based on it for the classroom wall.

- Each of these was a famous disaster from which only a handful of people survived:

  the eruption of Vesuvius in AD 79; the Massacre at Cawnpore in India in 1857; the sinking of the Titanic in 1912. Find out as much as you can about one or more of them, using the internet or reference books or both. Prepare a short presentation on your chosen topic(s) for the rest of the class or for a school assembly.

Chapter 3 Race

What do you think you're doing?

Sephy is a 'cross', a black girl, and her friend Callum is a 'nought' and white. In the world created by Malorie Blackman in this novel, crosses are superior and have all the advantages in society, although the two groups now attend the same schools and are, in theory, equal.

1 I lined up in the food queue. I wasn't going to do anything out of the ordinary, so why was my heart bumping in such a strange way? I collected my chicken and mushroom pie with the usual over-boiled trimmings, my jam tart with over-sweet custard and my carton of milk and, taking a deep
5 breath, I headed for Callum's table. Callum and the other noughts glanced up as I approached their table, only to look away again immediately.

'D'you mind if I join you?'

They all looked so shocked, it wasn't even funny. The other noughts continued to look stunned, but Callum's expression turned. I sat down
10 before he could say no and before I could bottle out.

'What d'you think you're doing?' he snapped.

'Eating my lunch,' I replied before cutting into my pie. I tried to smile at the other three noughts but they instantly returned to eating their food.

'Hi. I'm Sephy Hadley.' I thrust my hand under the nose of the nought girl I
15 was sitting next to. She had a dark brown plaster on her forehead which stuck out on her pale white skin like a throbbing thumb. 'Welcome to Heathcroft.'

She looked at my hand like it was about to bite her. Wiping her own hand on her tunic, she then took mine and shook it slowly.

20 'I'm Shania,' she said softly.

'That's a pretty name. What does it mean?' I asked.

Shania shrugged. 'It doesn't mean anything.'

'My mother told me my name means "serene night",' I laughed. 'But Callum will tell you I'm anything but serene!'

25 Shania smiled at me. It was tentative and brief but at least it was genuine – while it lasted.

'How's your head?' I asked, pointing at the plaster.

30

'It's OK. It'll take more than a stone step to dent my head.'

35 I smiled. 'That plaster's a bit noticeable.'

'They don't sell pink plasters.
40 Only dark brown ones.' Shania shrugged.

My eyes
45 widened at that. I'd never really thought about it before, but she was right. I'd never seen any pink plasters. Plasters were the colour of us crosses, not the noughts.

'Sephy, just what d'you think you're doing?' Mrs Bawden, the deputy
50 headmistress, appeared from nowhere to scowl down at me.

'Pardon?'

'What're you doing?'

'I'm eating my lunch.' I frowned.

'Don't be facetious.'

55 'I'm not. I'm eating my lunch.'

'Get back to your own table – at once.' Mrs Bawden looked like she was about to erupt kittens.

I looked around. I was now the centre of attention – the very last thing I'd wanted.

60 'B-but I'm sitting h-here,' I stammered.

'Get back to your own table – NOW!'

What table? I didn't have my own table. And then it dawned on me exactly what Mrs Bawden meant. She wasn't talking about me getting back to my own table. She was talking about me getting back to my own kind. I glanced
65 around. Callum and the others weren't looking at me. Everyone else was. They weren't.

'I'm sitting with my friend, Callum,' I whispered. I could hardly hear my own voice so I have no idea how Mrs Bawden heard me – but she did. She grabbed my arm and pulled me out of my chair. I was still holding on to my
70 tray, and everything on it went flying.

'Persephone Hadley, you will come with me.' Mrs Bawden yanked me away from the table and dragged me across the food hall. I tried to twist away from her, but she had a grip like a python on steroids. I turned my head this way and that. Wasn't anyone going to do anything? Not from the look of it. I
75 twisted sharply to look at Callum. He was watching but the moment I caught his eye, he looked away. I stopped struggling after that. I straightened up and followed Mrs Bawden to the headmaster's office.

Callum had turned away from me. I didn't care about the rest but I cared about that. He'd turned away … . Well, I was slow getting the message, but
80 I'd finally got it. God knows, I'd finally got it.

*　　*　　*

Callum

I had to get out of there. I left my lunch half-eaten and walked out of the food hall without saying a word to any of the others.

I had to get out of there.

85 I walked out of the food hall and out of the building and out of the school, my steps growing ever faster and more frantic – until by the time I was out of the school gates, I was running. Running until my back ached and my feet hurt and my heart was ready to burst and still I kept running. I ran all the way out of the town and down to the beach. I collapsed onto the cool sand,
90 my body bathed in sweat. I lay on my stomach and punched the sand. And again, and again. Until my knuckles were red raw and bleeding.

From *Noughts and Crosses* by Malorie Blackman (2001)

EXERCISE 3.1

Answer these questions. Quote from the passage in your answers:

1. Explain the meaning of (a) tentative (line 25), (b) facetious (line 54), (c) erupt (line 57).

2. Why does Sephy sit with Callum and his nought friends?

3. Why do you think Malorie Blackman makes Sephy tell you in detail what food she has on her tray?

4. Explain the significance of Shania's sticking plaster.

5. Comment on the comparisons 'like a throbbing thumb' (line 16) and 'like a python on steroids' (line 73). What do they show you about Sephy's character?

6. What is the 'message' which Sephy eventually 'gets' (lines 79 and 80)?

7. Why do you think Callum reacts as he does? What is he feeling?

I have a dream

Doctor Martin Luther King, Jr. was a black American clergyman who led a massive campaign for equal rights for black people, especially in the southern states of the US. This extract is from a famous speech he made in 1963 in Washington DC. Five years later he was assassinated in Memphis, Tennessee.

1   I am not unmindful that some of you have come here out of great trials and tribulations. Some of you have come fresh from narrow jail cells. Some of you have come from areas where your quest for freedom left you battered by the storms of persecution and staggered by the winds of police brutality.
5   You have been the veterans of creative suffering. Continue to work with the faith that unearned suffering is redemptive.

Go back to Mississippi, go back to Alabama, go back to South Carolina, go back to Georgia, go back to Louisiana, go back to the slums and ghettoes of our northern cities, knowing that somehow this situation can and will be
10   changed. Let us not wallow in the valley of despair.

I say to you today, my friends, that in spite of the difficulties and frustrations of the moment I still have a dream. It is a dream deeply rooted in the American dream.

I have a dream that one day this nation will rise up and live out the true
15   meaning of its creed: 'We hold these truths to be self-evident; that all men are created equal.'

I have a dream that one day on the red hills of Georgia the sons of former slaves and the sons of former
20   slave owners will be able to sit down together at the table of brotherhood.

I have a dream that one day even the state of Mississippi, a desert state
25   sweltering with the heat of injustice and oppression, will be transformed into an oasis of freedom and justice.

I have a dream that my four little children will one day live in a nation
30   where they will not be judged by the colour of their skin but by the content of their character.

I have a dream today.

I have a dream that one day every
35   valley shall be exalted, every hill and mountain shall be made low, the rough places will be made plains and

This statue of Martin Luther King, Jr. is located in Washington, D.C.

the crooked places will be made straight, and the glory of the Lord shall be revealed, and all flesh shall see it together.

40   This is our hope. This is the faith with which I return to the south. With this faith we will be able to hew out of the mountain of despair a stone of hope. With this faith we will be able to transform the jangling discords of our nation into a beautiful symphony of brotherhood. With this faith we will be able to work together, to pray together, to struggle together, to go to jail
45   together, to stand up for freedom together, knowing that we will be free one day.

From a speech made by Martin Luther King, Jr. (August 1963)

EXERCISE 3.2

Answer these questions. Refer closely to the passage in your answers:

1. In which American state did black people have the hardest time, according to Martin Luther King?

2. Explain the meaning of (a) veterans (line 5), (b) ghettoes (line 8), (c) creed (line 15), (d) exalted (line 35).

3. Sum up Dr King's hopes for the future in not more than two sentences.

4. What do you think Dr King means by (a) 'unearned suffering is redemptive' (line 6), (b) 'a beautiful symphony of brotherhood' (line 43)?

5. If you hadn't been told that Dr King was a clergyman how could you tell from (a) what he says and (b) the way he says it?

6. In what ways does the style of this speech – meant to be heard – differ from a persuasive opinion written to be read silently in, for example, a newspaper?

7. Why does Dr King repeat himself so often? Do you find it effective?

'Telephone Conversation'

1   The price seemed reasonable, location
      Indifferent. The landlady swore she lived
      Off premises. Nothing remained
      But self-confession. 'Madam,' I warned,
5   'I hate a wasted journey – I am African.'
      Silence. Silenced transmission of
      Pressurised good-breeding. Voice, when it came,
      Lipstick coated, long gold-rolled
      Cigarette-holder pipped. Caught I was, foully.
10   'HOW DARK?' ... I had not misheard ... 'ARE YOU LIGHT
      OR VERY DARK?' Button B. Button A[1]. Stench
      Of rancid breath of public hide-and-speak.
      Red booth. Red pillar-box. Red double-tiered
      Omnibus squelching tar. It was real! Shamed
15   By ill-mannered silence, surrender

Pushed dumbfounded to beg simplification.
Considerate she was, varying the emphasis –
'ARE YOU DARK? OR VERY LIGHT?' Revelation came.
'You mean – like plain or milk chocolate?'
20   Her assent was clinical, crushing in its light
Impersonality. Rapidly, wave-length adjusted,
I chose. 'West African sepia[2]' and as afterthought,
'Down in my passport.' Silence for spectroscopic
Flight of fancy, till truthfulness clanged her accent
25   Hard on the mouthpiece. 'WHAT'S THAT?' conceding
'DON'T KNOW WHAT THAT IS.' 'Like brunette.'
'THAT'S DARK, ISN'T IT?' 'Not altogether.
Facially, I am brunette, but, madam, you should see
The rest of me. Palm of my hand, soles of my feet
30   Are a peroxide[3] blond. Friction, caused –
Foolishly, madam – by sitting down, has turned
My bottom raven black – One moment, madam!' – sensing
Her receiver rearing on the thunderclap
About my ears – 'Madam,' I pleaded, 'wouldn't you rather
35   See for yourself?'

Wole Soyinka

Notes:
[1] Buttons A and B were part of the telephone system in call boxes before the introduction of automatic connection.
[2] Pale brown dye extracted from cuttle fish and used to tint old photographs
[3] Chemical used to turn dark hair light

Poetry technique: irony

Irony is the humorous or mildly sarcastic use of words to mean the opposite of what they normally mean.

Look at 'nothing remained / But self-confession' and 'Considerate she was' in 'Telephone Conversation' for example.

Compare these lines from 'Death of an Aircraft':

> Too young for bullets if not for bail
> But the other two were in prime condition
> To take on a load of ammunition.

What is Causley's point? Practise expressing his view in your own words without the use of irony.

EXERCISE 3.3

Read the poem 'Telephone Conversation' and then answer these questions as fully as you can. Quote from the poem in your answers:

1. Why does the narrator 'confess' to the woman that he is African (line 5)?

2. In what way does her reaction surprise him?

3. Explain the meaning of (a) pressurised (line 7), (b) rancid (line 12), (c) assent (line 20).

4. What evidence is there in the poem to show that this conversation took place in the 1950s or 1960s?

5. List all the words or phrases which describe colour in the poem.

6. What do you deduce from the poem about the educational background of (a) the narrator and (b) the woman? Give reasons.

7. Why does he mention his bottom?

8. What features make 'Telephone Conversation' a poem rather than a story?

Your turn to write

EXERCISE 3.4

1. Sephy and Callum in *Noughts and Crosses* are very close friends. Imagine the next time they meet privately and describe what happens and what they say to each other.

2. Imagine you are the woman phoned by the narrator of Wole Soyinka's poem. Write your version of what happened as if you were writing a letter to a friend. Develop her personality in any way you wish.

3. Write about race in any way you wish.

4. Write a poem or story of your own entitled 'Telephone Call'.

5. Write a persuasive speech on any subject you wish. Use some of the methods used by Martin Luther King and remember that a good speech is very different in style and tone from an essay.

6. Write a story called 'A Stone of Hope'.

Writing workshop

Dialogue in stories

Most fiction includes passages, sometimes quite long ones, in which two or more characters are in conversation – or dialogue. Most of the extract from *Noughts and Crosses*, for example, is based on dialogue.

The skill is (a) to find a way of making

your characters speak in a way which shows the reader what these people are like and (b) to make it convincing.

The best way to develop this double-edged skill is to look closely and analytically at the dialogue in any fiction book you read and notice how the author is presenting it.

Some points and possibilities:

- Today it is usual to begin the words of a new speaker on a new line – open plan punctuation – but it wasn't always done this way. Look at any novel by Jane Austen (1775–1817), for example, to see how dialogue used to be presented.

- In modern, conventional fictional dialogue spoken words are marked off from the rest of the sentence or paragraph with single or double inverted commas – although a number of very successful 'experimental' authors have tried doing it in other ways: James Joyce (1892–1941) in *A Portrait of the Artist as a Young Man* (1916) for instance.

- The reader has to know who is speaking. That usually means statements such as 'he said' 'she agreed' or 'shouted Peter'. These can come before, after or in the middle of the words spoken and good writers vary the pattern all the time to keep the story flowing and lively.

- You can use adverbs such as 'emphatically', 'vehemently' or 'softly' if you want to stress the way the character is speaking.

- You can also use – and this is usually better (although take care not to overdo it) – very carefully chosen verbs such as 'opined', 'bellowed', 'suggested', 'whispered' or 'muttered' instead of a more general verb with an adverb.

- If only two people are speaking, and it is clear to the reader which is which, you can sometimes omit the explanatory words. This makes the dialogue flow faster and can be useful for things such as arguments in which characters are responding to each other very quickly.

EXERCISE 3.5

1. Reread the *Noughts and Crosses* passage in this chapter looking closely at how Malorie Blackman has managed the dialogue, bearing in mind the points listed above. It might help to discuss this with a partner.

2. Now write a fictional dialogue of your own, as if it were part of a story, in which three characters have a disagreement or misunderstanding.

Grammar and punctuation

Conjunctions

Conjunctions are joining words. (Remember that a junction on a railway line is a joining place.)

They can join two or more short sentences together to make one (differently punctuated) longer sentence or they can join ideas or words within a sentence.

The following can all be used as conjunctions:

because	although	whereas	since	and
but	as	while	or	until
despite	however	after	before	yet
though	notwithstanding	nonetheless		

Add to this list yourself. Watch for them in your reading and make yourself aware of how they work.

Try to use conjunctions imaginatively in your writing. You don't always have to use the most obvious one.

EXERCISE 3.6

Write out the following sentences putting conjunctions in the spaces:

1. Martin Luther King was an impressive speaker _____ not everyone liked what he said.

2. Wole Soyinka, a fine poet _____ playwright, _____ won the Nobel prize for Literature in 1986.

3. _____ her good intentions Sephy Hadley showed Callum up in a public place.

4. _____ I have finished *Noughts and Crosses* I want to read the sequel *Knife Edge*.

5. Malorie Blackman wrote *Noughts and Crosses* _____ Beverley Naidoo wrote *Out of Bounds*.

6. Wole Soyinka's poem is enjoyable _____ I usually prefer more traditional poetry.

Demonstrative and relative pronouns

A **pronoun** is a word which stands in place of a noun. There are various sorts of pronoun. Here are two which may be new to you.

A **demonstrative pronoun** is one which indicates (or demonstrates) precisely which one of something is meant. Think of it as being accompanied by a gesture. There are four in Standard English:

> **this**   **these**   **that**   **those**

(You might hear or read others such as 'yon' or 'yonder' in Scotland.)

> I like **this**.
> **These** are my favourites.
> **That** is the best.
> **Those** are worst.

Alternatively, they can be used, like adjectives, in front of nouns to modify them:

> **This** book is brilliant.
> **Those** plums are sour.
> Did you see **that** car?
> Put **these** papers away.

A **relative pronoun** is one which introduces a subordinate clause (see Chapter 6) in a sentence and refers to a noun which has gone before it in the sentence. '**Who**', '**whom**', '**which**' and '**that**' are the commonest:

> This is the boy **who** is coming to supper tomorrow.

('who is coming to supper tomorrow' is a subordinate clause and 'who' points back to the noun 'boy')

> Wole Soyinka comes from Nigeria, **which** is in West Africa.

('which is in West Africa' is a subordinate clause and 'which' looks back to 'Nigeria')

> My uncle, to **whom** I owe a great deal, has died.

('to whom I owe a great deal' is a subordinate clause and 'whom' refers to 'uncle')

Remember to use 'whom' when you would otherwise say 'him' or 'them'.

(If you learn Latin, you will know (I'm sure) to use 'whom' with the accusative, genitive, dative and ablative cases.)

The '-m' at the end of both words is significant:

> My uncle has died. I owe a great deal to **him**.

And use 'whom' after the prepositions 'by', 'with' or 'from':

> My granny, from **whom** I learnt to cook, lives in Somerset.

> Martin Luther King lived with his wife, by **whom** he had four children.

> Sephy Hadley admired Callum, with **whom** she tried to share a table.

The noun in the sentence to which the relative pronoun refers in all these examples is called, in grammar, the **antecedent**.

EXERCISE 3.7

Put demonstrative or relative pronouns in the spaces in these sentences. Write in brackets after each sentence which sort of pronoun(s) you have used:

1. My brother, _____ hates cabbage, actually ate some when he was away at camp.

2. Shall I put the books on _____ shelf or on _____ one?

3. _____ is my pen.

4. I like _____ dress.

5. We still have all the glasses _____ my parents were given as a wedding present.

6. Wole Soyinka, to _____ many fine tributes have been written, was 70 in 2004.

7. My aunt, with _____ my uncle raised a large family, is a wonderful mother.

8. We seem to have hotter summers _____ days.

Commas

Remember that a sentence is a closed box starting with a **capital letter** and ending with a **full stop, question mark** or **exclamation mark**. Commas can be used only inside the box (see Chapter 2). Commas are often a matter of choice and taste. Many commas are optional. The general trend now is to use fewer commas rather than more, but sometimes they are necessary within a sentence to make the grammar and meaning clear.

EXERCISE 3.8

Add commas to these sentences:

1. If it is fine tomorrow I should like to play cricket.

2. Although I have read many of Wole Soyinka's poems I have yet to see any of his plays.

3. When I saw how tired she looked I decided not to tell her of our plans but she asked me about them saying how interested she was so I had no choice.

4. In May this year Emma Courtenay joined our school as a member of Year 7 and as she loves maths she is actively looking for ways of doing more getting really good marks and taking GCSE early.

5. Meanwhile Mrs Bawden had crept up on Sephy silent and determined.

6. Shall we pack up now carry on for a bit longer take a break or get ourselves a drink of tea coffee or juice to sip while we're working?

Spell check: -y/-ies (nouns)

To form the plural of nouns which end with '-y' we usually change the 'y' to 'ies' when the letter before the '-y' is a **consonant**. So:

opportunity	opportun**ies**
baby	bab**ies**
nursery	nurser**ies**
jelly	jell**ies**

With nouns which have a **vowel** before the '-y' we simply add 's' in the plural. So:

monkey	monkey**s**
boy	boy**s**
quay	quay**s**

An exception to this is 'money' whose plural is 'monies' – a technical term generally used in banking and law.

EXERCISE 3.9

Write the correctly spelt plurals of the following words:

laboratory	lady	fly	buoy	kidney
alloy	apology	entry	Monday	symphony

EXERCISE 3.10

Check that you can spell these ten words taken from the three passages in this chapter:

immediately	collapsed	stomach	premises	surrender
emphasis	chocolate	adjusted	conceding	receiver

What do you notice about the spelling of 'facetious'? This is very unusual in English.

Vocabulary

-scope words

'Spectroscopic', which originally referred to a scientific instrument the spectroscope, means 'visually wide ranging'. It was formed in the 19th century from the Latin word *spectrum* ('something seen') and the Greek word *scopeo* ('to look at').

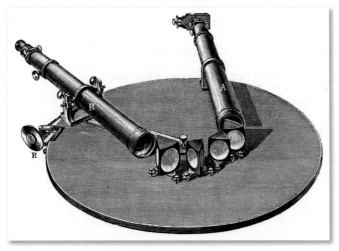

The spectroscope (also known as a spectrometer) is used by scientists to measure properties of light

EXERCISE 3.11

What do these words mean? Try to work them out for yourself if they are new to you. Then use a dictionary to check:

1. scope
2. telescope
3. microscope
4. kaleidoscope
5. periscope
6. stethoscope
7. spectrum
8. spectral
9. spectacle
10. spectate

EXERCISE 3.12

'Redemptive' is the adjective formed from the verb 'to redeem' and the linked noun 'redemption'.

Use the following forms of words, which may not be familiar to you, in sentences of your own, to show that you understand their meaning:

1. discursive (adjective from the verb 'to discuss' and the noun 'discussion')
2. condemnation (noun from the verb 'to condemn')
3. illustrative (adjective from the verb 'to illustrate' and the noun 'illustration')
4. illusory (adjective from the noun 'illusion')
5. opportune (adjective from the noun 'opportunity')
6. severity (noun from the adjective 'severe')
7. adjectival (adjective from the noun 'adjective')
8. quantify (verb from the noun 'quantity')
9. opine (verb from the noun 'opinion')
10. ascertain (verb from the adjective 'certain')

Speaking and listening

1. Work with a partner on Wole Soyninka's 'Telephone Call'. One of you should read the narrator's part and the other the woman's. When you're satisfied with your work, join up with another pair and listen to each other's interpretation.

2. Working in a pair, develop a telephone conversation in which the speakers are disagreeing or misunderstand each other. Choose any subject you wish.

3. Read Martin Luther King Jr.'s speech aloud several times to feel its rhythms. What do you notice about the speed you are using? Work out why this is. Then listen to a recording of Luther King saying these words (easily available via the internet) and compare your performance with his.

4. Work in a group of four. Discuss why you think there is so much racial tension in different parts of the world. What could be done to make things better? When you've finished your discussion, a spokesperson for your group should summarise your group's views for the rest of the class.

5. Read one of the books in 'Have you read?' Tell the rest of the class about it.

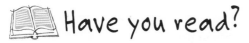 Have you read?

All these books have racial themes:

*   *Noughts and Crosses* by Malorie Blackman (2001)
*   *Boys Don't Cry* by Malorie Blackman (2010)
*   *Out of Bounds* by Beverley Naidoo (2001)
*   *The Joy Luck Club* by Amy Tan (1989)
*   *Things Fall Apart* by Chinua Achebe (1958)
*   *One More River* by Lynne Reid Banks (1973)
*   *Across the Barricades* by Joan Lingard (1972)
*   *To Kill a Mockingbird* by Harper Lee (1960)
*   *To Sir With Love* by E R Braithwaite (1959)
*   *A Wedding Man is Nicer Than Cats, Miss* by Rachel Scott (1971)
*   *Purple Hibiscus* by Chimamanda Ngozi Adichie (2003)
*   *Anita and Me* by Meera Syal (1996)

✔ And if you've done all that ...

- Find out what you can about the American Civil Rights movement in the 1960s from books and the internet. Develop your findings into a short presentation for the rest of the class.

- Benjamin Zephaniah and Grace Nicholls are well-known British black poets. Read some of their poems and create your own anthology of your favourites.

- Work with a partner. Write a short play in which race is a theme. Newspapers can be useful sources of story ideas.

- In 2007/8 The Royal Shakespeare Company presented a version of *Noughts and Crosses* as a stage play. There is information relating to this on the RSC website and you can watch extracts from the play. Look at some of this material as a way of exploring the novel and Malorie Blackman's ideas further: www.rsc.org.uk

Chapter 4 Christmas

Carol singers

It is Christmas Eve in the early 19th century in the village of Mellstock (loosely based on the Dorset villages of Stinsford and Lower Bockhampton). Carol singers, and the traditional musicians who accompanied hymns in church before organs were usual, known collectively as 'the choir', are doing their annual rounds.

1 An increasing light made itself visible in one of the windows of the upper floor. It came so close to the blind that the exact position of the flame could be perceived from the outside. Remaining steady for an instant the blind went upward from before it, revealing to thirty concentrated eyes a
5 young girl framed as a picture by the window architrave[1] and unconsciously illuminating her countenance to a vivid brightness by a candle she held in her left hand, close to her face. She was wrapped in a white robe of some kind, whilst down her shoulders fell a twining profusion of marvellously rich hair, in a wild disorder which proclaimed it to be only during the night that
10 such a condition was discoverable. Her bright eyes were looking into the gray world outside with an uncertain expression, oscillating between courage and shyness which, as she recognised the semicircular group of dark forms gathered before her, transformed itself into pleasant resolution.

Opening the window, she said lightly and warmly:

15 'Thank you, singers, thank you!'

Together went the window quickly and quietly and the blind started downward on its return to its place. Her fair forehead and eyes vanished; her little mouth; her neck and shoulders; all of her. Then the spot of candlelight shone nebulously as before; then it moved away.

20 'How pretty!' exclaimed Dick Dewy.

'If she'd been rale waxwork she couldn't ha been comelier,' said Michael Mail.

'As near a thing to a spiritual vision as ever I wish to see,' said tranter[2] Dewy fervently.

25 All the rest, after clearing their throats and adjusting their hats, agreed that such a sight was worth singing for.

'Now to Farmer Shinar's, and then replenish our insides, Father,' said the tranter.

'Wi' all my heart,' said old William, shouldering his bass-viol[3].

30 Farmer Shinar's was a queer lump of a house, standing at the corner of a lane that ran obliquely into the principal thoroughfare. The upper windows were much wider than they were high, and this feature, together with a broad bay window where the door might have been expected, gave it by day the aspect of a human countenance turned askance, and wearing a sly
35 and wicked leer.

'Forty breaths and number thirty two – "Behold the
40 morning star"!' said old William.

They had reached the
45 end of the second verse and the fiddlers were doing the up
50 stroke previously to pouring forth the opening chord of the
55 third verse, when, without a light appearing or any signal
60 being given, a roaring voice exclaimed:

'Shut up! Don't make your blaring row here. A feller wi' a headache enough to split likes a quiet night.'

Slam went the window.

65 'Hullo, that's an ugly blow for we artists!' said the tranter, in a keenly
appreciative voice and turning to his companions.

'Finish the carrel, all who be friends of harmony!' said old William
commandingly: and they continued to the end.

'Forty breaths and number nineteen!' said William firmly. 'Give it to him
well; the choir can't be insulted in this manner!'

70 A light now flashed into existence, the window opened, and the farmer
stood revealed as one in a terrific passion.

'Drown en! – drown en!' the tranter cried, fiddling frantically. 'Play fortissmy
and drown his spaking!'

'Fortissmy!' said Michael Mail, and the music and singing waxed so loud that
75 it was impossible to know what Mr Shinar had said, was saying or was
about to say: but wildly flinging his arms and body about in the form of
capital Xs and Ys, he appeared to utter enough invectives to consign the
whole parish to perdition.

'Very unseemly – very!' said old William, as they retired. 'Never such a
80 dreadful scene in the whole round o' my carrel practice – never!'

They now crossed the Twenty-Acres to proceed to the lower village, and
met Voss with the hot mead and bread and cheese as they were crossing
the churchyard. This determined them to eat and drink before proceeding
further, and they entered the belfry[4]. The lanterns were opened and the
85 whole body sat round against the walls on benches and whatever else was
available and made a hearty meal. In the pauses of conversation could be
heard throughout the floor overhead a little world of undertones and
creaks from the halting clockwork which never spread further than the
tower they were born in.

90 Having done eating and drinking, the instruments were again tuned, and
once more the party emerged into the night air.

'Where's Dick?' said old Dewy.

Every man looked round him upon every other man as if Dick might have
been transmuted into one or the other: and then they said that they didn't
95 know.

'He've clinked off home-along, depend upon't!' suggested one of the men.

'I hope no fatal tragedy has overtook the lad!' said his grandfather.

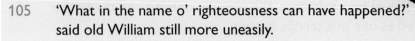

'O no,' replied tranter Dewy placidly. 'Wonder where he've put that there
100 fiddle of his. Why that fiddle cost thirty shillens, and good words besides. Somewhere in the damp, without doubt; that there instrument will be unglued and spoilt in ten minutes.'

105 'What in the name o' righteousness can have happened?' said old William still more uneasily.

Adapted from *Under the Greenwood Tree* by Thomas Hardy (1872)

Notes:
[1] A moulded frame around a window
[2] Someone who earned his living as a casual delivery man
[3] An old stringed instrument played wedged upright on the lap like a small 'cello
[4] Church tower with bells

EXERCISE 4.1

Answer the following questions as fully as you can. Quote from the passage in your answers:

1. Explain the meaning of (a) oscillating (line 11), (b) nebulously (line 19), (c) transmuted (line 94).

2. Find expressions in the passage which mean exactly the same as (a) eat a good meal, (b) to be swearing strongly, (c) joined the main road at an angle.

3. How many men were there in the choir?

4. Explain why the girl's hair was particularly fascinating.

5. Thomas Hardy was an architect by training. Which details in the passage show his interest?

6. Explain why William insists that the choir sing and play on outside Farmer Shinar's house.

7. What do you think has happened to Dick?

8. Thomas Hardy was an amateur violinist. How might you have guessed that from this passage?

Christmas and the Red Cross

This piece of writing describes how a well known charity's policy on Christmas decorations was criticised by cultural commentators.

1   In 1863, a Swiss businessman, Henry Dunant had a radical idea for a new international movement. He wanted an organisation which, in times of war, would aid the wounded and dying, who would otherwise be left to suffer. Dunant's initial idea quickly gained influence. In the same year the
5   International Committee of the Red Cross (ICRC) was formed in Geneva. Its job would be to coordinate the efforts of similar groups in other countries in order to change attitudes across the world.

Dunant continued his work in the movement. He was involved in the signing of the original Geneva Convention (1864). Twelve European
10 countries signed the agreement, consisting of 10 Articles. The Articles were meant to protect casualties of war but also those people who provide medical aid on and off the battlefield.

Today the ICRC is still based in Switzerland and continues to lead the movement. It is supported by the Internal Federation of Red Cross and Red
15 Crescent Societies (IFRC), which is made up of the 187 separate Red Cross and Red Crescent organisations around the world. The Red Crescent is used as an alternative symbol for the Red Cross in countries where Islam is more popular than Christianity.

The Geneva Convention has also been expanded several times since it was
20 started. The present Geneva Conventions consist of four major treaties and three extra aggreements called protocols. Most countries in the world are signatories. And the work of The Red Cross is no longer limited to war areas. They respond to both natural and man-made disasters, provide social care and offer first aid training.

25 In 1965, The Red Cross issued its seven fundamental principles. One of the principles is a commitment to remain neutral in conflicts. This includes military conflicts but also clashes of political, cultural and religious ideology. Alix Miller, writing on the official blog of the British Red Cross in 2010, explained the reason for the principle of neutrality:

30 'Often we provide help in countries that other organisations cannot or will not work in.'

'We cross front lines in times of war to help conflict victims and visit

prisoners of war on both sides. We can only do this life-saving work because we are understood to be a completely neutral, independent
35   organisation. Put simply, our neutrality saves lives.'

Alix was responding to a news story which challenged the Red Cross's neutrality. The story was covered by several news organisations. It was originally circulated in 2002 when the events described first occurred, and then unexpectedly again in 2010. Various media groups became confused
40   about whether the story was current or historical, and so the story was covered again as if it was news.

A particular version of the story by the *Daily Mail*, still available to read on their website (now correctly dated 2002) was sensationally titled 'The Red Cross bans Christmas'. The writer, Steve Doughty, described what he saw as
45   a widespread and strongly negative reaction (a 'furore') to the Red Cross's ruling on Christmas decorations. According to Doughty, the Red Cross had decided not to include any religious decorations in their store displays because 'they could offend Moslems'.

Doughty quoted Christine Banks, a store volunteer, who said she thought
50   the policy was 'offensive to Moslems' as well as to her. Lord Ahmed (a Muslim politician) called it 'stupid'. Rod Thomas (a vicar) joked 'they should start calling themselves The Red Splodge'. And Major Charles Heyman (editor of *Janes World Armies*[1] from 1995–2003) made the point that celebrating Christmas 'could hardly upset' the Red Cross's important work
55   of running prisoner-of-war programmes and relief efforts for civilians.

Doughty made the impression that the Red Cross's policy was a petty example of political correctness and a pointless gesture. He felt that the negative reaction from these public figures was 'a fresh blow to the image of what was once one of Britain's most respected charities'.

60   But the Red Cross say their store policy on decorations fits with their principle of neutrality. They say decorations of an 'overtly religious nature' have never been permitted, and nothing changed in 2002. In her blog post, Alix Miller argued that abandoning neutrality, even when some might consider it trivial, can have a powerful and long-term effect. She concluded
65   that: 'in a world where information travels quickly and pervasively – a world where an eight-year-old news story is still raising questions with our supporters – we have to make sure we act consistently across the board.'

Christopher Scrace (2012)

Notes: [1] A publication concerned with military activity around the world

EXERCISE 4.2

Read the article above, then answer the following questions:

1. What is the policy of the Red Cross on Christmas decorations in its stores?

2. Find words in the passage which mean the same as (a) impartiality, (b) row, (c) unimportant.

3. Apart from providing aid in war time, what work is the Red Cross involved in today?

4. What is the name of the equivalent organisation to the Red Cross for Moslems?

5. Why were the views of Major Charles Heyman included in the article by the *Daily Mail*?

6. Is the above piece of writing unbiased, or is the author trying to present a particular point of view? Give reasons for your answer.

'Christmas'

1   The bells of waiting Advent ring,
      The Tortoise stove[1] is lit again
    And lamp-oil light across the night
      Has caught the streaks of winter rain
5   In many a stained-glass window sheen
    From Crimson Lake to Hooker's Green.

    The holly in the windy hedge
      And round the Manor House the yew
    Will soon be stripped to deck the ledge,
10   The altar, font and arch and pew,
    So that the villagers can say
    'The church looks nice' on Christmas Day.

Provincial public-houses blaze
    And Corporation tramcars clang,
15   On lighted tenements I gaze
    Where paper decorations hang,
And bunting in the red Town Hall
Says 'Merry Christmas to you all'.

And London shops on Christmas Eve
20   Are strung with silver bells and flowers
As hurrying clerks the city leave
    To pigeon-haunted classic towers,
And marbled clouds go scudding by
The many-steepled London sky.

25   And girls in slacks remember Dad,
        And oafish louts remember Mum,
    And sleepless children's hearts are glad,
        And Christmas-morning bells say 'Come!'
    Even to shining ones who dwell
30   Safe in the Dorchester Hotel.

    And is it true? And is it true,
        This most tremendous tale of all,
    Seen in a stained glass window's hue,
        A Baby in an ox's stall?
35   The Maker of the stars and sea
    Became a Child on earth for me?

    And is it true? For if it is,
        No loving fingers tying strings
    Around those tissued fripperies,
40   The sweet and silly Christmas things,
    Bath salts and inexpensive scent
    And hideous tie so kindly meant,

    No love that in a family dwells,
        No carolling in frosty air,
45   Nor all the steeple-shaking bells
        Can with this simple truth compare –
    That God was Man in Palestine
    And lives today in Bread and Wine.

John Betjeman (1958)

Notes:
[1] A small fuel-burning stove used for heating

Poetry technique: rhyme

Rhyme is the use of words which have endings which sound the same, such as 'dwells' and 'bells' or 'clang' and 'hang'. It applies to sound not spelling, so 'air' rhymes with 'compare'.

It can also apply to more than one syllable as in 'flowers' and 'towers' or, in 'Death of an Aircraft', 'stations' and 'relations' and 'condition' and 'ammunition'.

Poets frequently rhyme their line endings, sometimes in lines which follow each other and sometimes in lines which are further apart. In verse one of 'Christmas', for example, Betjeman rhymes 'again' with 'rain', and 'sheen' with 'green'. Oddly, there is no rhyme to link the first with the third line, although he does rhyme the first and third in all other verses.

Look carefully at the pattern of the rhyme scheme in verse one of 'Christmas' and compare it with the rhyme scheme in the other verses. Then compare it with the pattern in 'Circus Lion' and 'Death of an Aircraft'. Try to work out what effect the rhyme has on the meaning of the poem.

Sometimes poets also use rhyme to link words which are not at the ends of lines. 'Light' and 'night' rhyme in the third line of verse 1 for instance. This is known as **internal rhyme**.

Poetry like 'Telephone Conversation', which doesn't have rhymed line endings, is called **blank verse**. Blank verse is also the term used for the kind of unrhymed scheme used by Shakespeare (see Chapter 5 on iambic pentameter).

EXERCISE 4.3

Read the poem 'Christmas' and then answer these questions. Quote from the poem in your answer.

1. What pre-Christmas preparations are described in the poem?

2. What is the meaning of (a) Advent (line 1), (b) Corporation (line 14), (c) tenements (line 15)?

3. Which details in the poem tell you that this poem was written in and about the 1950s?

4. What do you think the poet is trying to say? Sum up the poem's message in your own words.

5. Look carefully at the poem's rhyme pattern. What does this add to the poem?

6. Comment on the phrases (a) 'pigeon-haunted classic towers' (line 22), (b) 'hideous tie so kindly meant' (line 42).

Your turn to write

EXERCISE 4.4

1. Write a story or poem about any aspect of Christmas you wish.

2. Write a nativity story – or play – set in your community today.

3. Write a short essay in response to the following statement: 'It is important not to offend people who hold different religious beliefs to yourself'.

4. Imagine you are either the girl at the window or Farmer Shinar in Thomas Hardy's Mellstock. Write a letter to a friend describing the visit of the carollers. Invent as much detail as you like.

5. Some people argue that Christmas now focuses so much on buying things like presents, decorations and elaborate food that it has lost its true meaning. Do you agree? Write your views.

6. Describe the celebration of Christmas in your school or in a school you have attended in the past. Make your writing as lively as you can.

Writing workshop

Writing a play script

Most plays consist mostly of actors speaking (and/or singing) words which have been written for them by playwrights or lyricists. In many ways it is similar to the dialogue in novels we looked at in Chapter 3 but, as you probably know, it is usually set down differently.

Play scripts usually include:

- descriptive blocks of stage directions describing the set, atmosphere and indicating where and how the characters are placed on the stage

- the names of the characters as they speak in bold type or block capitals down the left hand margin of the page, often followed by a colon (:)

- the words spoken by the characters which are set out after the character's name

- short stage directions in italics or brackets to indicate when a character enters or leaves (exits) the stage. They also often tell the actor, for example, how a character might speak, what he or she might be doing or thinking or anything else which the playwright thinks will help the actor to interpret the character as the playwright wants.

A field. Dawn, 5 August, 1914. War was declared by the Prime Minister and Cabinet in London at 11 p.m. on the previous day.

Enter Ned, spying. Goose begins to stalk him.

Joey messes up again.

In a foreshadowing of the episode that occurs later when Joey inspires the gun team, he finds the resources from deep inside to pull the plough.

Descriptive block of stage directions

Albert   That's it, dig in, dig in, and pull! And pull! You're getting it, you're getting it. Good boy, Joey! Good boy, Joey! Good boy!

Joey suddenly loses his footing and slips over.

Short stage direction

Get up! Get up, Joey! You've got to get up! Joey, you don't know, so I'm going to have to do the knowing for you, that the rest of your life depends on this. So get set to pull straight.

Goose flushes Ned out of hiding.

Albert   Spying?

Words spoken by characters

Ned   Waiting vor vather.

Albert   'Waiting vor vather.'

Names of characters in bold type

Ned   I didn't zay it like that, ya little runt.

Albert   Runt? It takes one ta know one.

Ned   Enjoy your last few minutes with that horse.

From *War Horse* by Nick Stafford (1982) (based on the novel by Michael Morpurgo)

When you write a play script, you should do the following:

- Keep the characters' speeches fairly short. You want it to sound realistic. In real life most people don't make long speeches.

- Remember that people often interrupt each other.

- Have a clear idea of what you want your characters to be doing and set it out explicitly for your actors.

- Get a group of friends to read through your work as a play reading. Change anything which doesn't flow or feel right.

EXERCISE 4.5

1. Choose a section of the extract from *Under the Greenwood Tree* which starts this chapter and adapt it as a mini-play. Use all the conventions for setting out a play script. Make your stage directions clear. Remember that adapters do not have to use the exact words spoken by the characters in the novel.

2. Write a scene of a play which relates to Christmas in some way. You could do this either working on your own or in a pair.

Grammar and punctuation

Prepositions

A **preposition** tells you where a noun or pronoun is in relation to something else in the sentence. Prepositions are words such as:

around	behind	above	near	into
through	opposite	from	across	towards

My friend lives **within** York's city walls.

Cameron had a letter **from** his mother.

We arranged our Christmas cards **along** the shelves.

Some prepositions need particular care:

among: Something is shared **among several** people.

between: Something is shared **between** two people.

beside means 'at the side of'. So: 'Henry stood **beside** the river.'

besides means 'in addition to'. So: 'Several boys were in the team **besides** Oliver.'

in shows the position in one place. So: 'Father Christmas was stuck **in** the chimney.'

into shows movement from one place to another. So: 'The reindeer tumbled **into** the garden.'

past is a preposition and is always used with a verb: 'The sleigh went **past** our house.' ('passed' is not a preposition but the past tense of the verb 'to pass'. So: 'The sleigh passed our house.')

EXERCISE 4.6

Make up sentences of your own, using the following prepositions. Remember that some of these words can also be used as other parts of speech. Your job here is to use them as prepositions:

1.	beyond	6.	without
2.	beside	7.	under
3.	during	8.	past
4.	after	9.	by
5.	among	10.	into

Articles

There are eight parts of speech (sometimes called word classes): **noun**, **verb**, **adverb**, **adjective**, **pronoun**, **conjunction**, **preposition** … and **article**.

Of these, the **article** is by far the simplest. Only three words in English are articles:

the   **a**   **an**

'The' is the **definite article** because '**the** pudding' or '**the** Christmas tree' means a **specific** one.

'A' is the **indefinite article** because '**a** pudding' or '**a** Christmas tree' refers to **any** one.

'An' is just another form of the indefinite article. It means exactly the same as 'a' but is used when the next word begins with a vowel as it is easier to say. So '**an** umbrella', '**an** elephant', '**an** enormous balloon', '**an** opened present'.

Sometimes 'an' is used before a word beginning with 'h', although this is becoming increasingly rare. For example you may find '**an** historian' or '**an** hotel'.

In each case, the article is modifying the noun which follows it by stating its definite or indefinite status.

EXERCISE 4.7

See how many words of four letters and more you can make out of the words:

DEFINITE ARTICLE

Punctuating direct speech

When you punctuate direct speech, enclose all the words spoken in **inverted commas** (also called **speech marks** or **quotation marks**). You usually also need a comma, full stop, question mark or exclamation mark at the end of the words spoken. Begin a new paragraph every time a new person speaks.

Look carefully at these examples:

'Now to Farmer Shinar's, and then replenish our insides, Father,' said the tranter.

'Very unseemly – very!' said old William, as they retired.

'Where's Dick?' said old Dewy.

'Forty breaths and number nineteen!' said William firmly. 'Give it to him well; the choir can't be insulted in this manner!'

EXERCISE 4.8

Write the following conversation with its correct punctuation:

Mr Pickwick is about to try ice skating.

It looks nice warm exercise that doesn't it he enquired of Wardle. Ah it does indeed replied Wardle. Do you slide? I used to do so on the gutters when I was a boy replied Mr Pickwick. Try it now said Wardle. Oh do please Mr Pickwick cried all the ladies. I should be very happy to afford you some amusement replied Mr Pickwick but I haven't done such a thing these thirty years.

From *Pickwick Papers* by Charles Dickens (1836–37)

Spell check: -y/-ies (verbs)

Verbs which end in '-y', if the letter before the '-y' is a **consonant** (like the nouns we looked at in Chapter 3) change the 'y' to 'ies' when we use that part of the verb which requires an 's'. So:

I deny	he den**ies**
We apply	she app**lies**
You defy	he def**ies**
I dry	it dr**ies**

Verbs which end in '-y' but which have a vowel before it simply add 's' as required. So:

I play	it play**s**
We buy	he buy**s**
You portray	she portray**s**
I enjoy	he enjoy**s**

EXERCISE 4.9

Write these sentences, adding the correctly spelt form of the given verb:

1. Peter (fry) eggs for breakfast but Jack (enjoy) mushrooms more.
2. 'We must make sure he (purify) the water,' said the desert explorer of an assistant.
3. Our cat (stray) further than we'd like him to.
4. The school (supply) pupils with stationery but each boy or girl (try) not to waste it.
5. That machine (amplify) the sound.
6. Laura (deny) that she (buy) sweets but Hatty (say) she has seen her do so.

EXERCISE 4.10

These 20 words are used in the three passages above. Carefully learn their spellings and then practise writing them in sentences:

perceived	concentrated	unconsciously	proclaimed	spiritual
obliquely	appreciative	existence	righteousness	tortoise
provincial	tremendous	inexpensive	neutrality	furore
signatories	ideology	circulated	gesture	pervasively

Vocabulary

-logy words

The word 'mythology' comes from the Greek words *muthos*, meaning 'fable', and *logos*, meaning 'word' or 'speech'. It means 'the body of knowledge and stories associated with a particular culture'.

A word ending with -logy or -ology usually now means the study of that subject. So we get words like 'zoology' which means 'the scientific study of animals' and 'psychology', 'the scientific study of the human mind'.

EXERCISE 4.11

Match the following -ology words to their meanings. Work out the ones which are obvious to you first and then use a dictionary to sort out the rest.

theology	study of birds
chronology	study of human beings
archaeology	study of the weather
neurology	study of the nature of God
ornithology	study of animals
musicology	study of history to establish dates
zoology	study of the human nervous system
anthropology	study of ancient history though excavation
meteorology	study of music as an academic subject

Which -ology is going on here?

Synonyms

Christopher Scrace wrote 'Among them is a *commitment* to remain neutral' when he could just as easily have used **synonyms** such as 'promise', 'pledge' or 'vow'.

English has many synonyms (words which are similar in meaning) but remember these two points:

1. Words change their meaning according to context, so that two words may mean something similar in one context but not in another. For example, 'beat' means the same as 'overcame' in the sentence 'I beat/overcame my fear' but you cannot say 'I counted her heart-overcame' or 'I'll overcome the eggs for the omelette'.

    For another example, 'book' is a synonym for 'reserve' if you say 'I must book/reserve a table in the restaurant' but you cannot say 'I want to change my library reserve' or 'She's the book for the netball team'.

You can make up lots of examples of this for yourself.

2. It is very unusual for two words to mean exactly the same as each other. 'Ordered' suggests that there was no choice or room for argument. 'Asked' would have meant something similar but that there was a possibility they might have refused.

EXERCISE 4.12

Provide as many synonyms as you can for the words in bold as they are used in these sentences. Try to do this without using a thesaurus:

1. Maria and Rasheed **walked** home.

2. John Betjeman **captures** the atmosphere of Christmas.

3. Christmas can be a **jolly** season.

4. I read **quickly**.

5. Our teacher insists on **courtesy** in the classroom.

6. When we saw the mess it was hard not to **giggle**.

Speaking and listening

1. As a class, find as many Christmas poems as you can. Learn and rehearse one each. Then organise a Christmas poetry festival in which you all speak and share your poems. You could invite another class to share this with you.

2. Organise a class discussion or debate about what Christmas means to you and what it should mean.

3. With adult permission and advice, interview an older person (one of your grandparents or great-grandparents, perhaps) about how Christmas was celebrated when he or she was young. Alternatively, find someone to interview who has spent his or her childhood in another country.

4. With your teacher's agreement, invite to your classroom someone with strong views about Christmas, perhaps a vicar, or a nurse who works over Christmas, or a shopkeeper who relies on the higher takings that Christmas brings. Prepare questions to ask your guest. One of the class should introduce him or her and another should sum up and thank the guest at the end.

Have you read?

These books are all either about Christmas or include Christmas as part of the story:

- *Under the Greenwood Tree* by Thomas Hardy (1872)
- *Puffin Book of Christmas Stories* ed. Wendy Cooling (2001)
- *Oxford Book of Christmas Stories* ed. Dennis Pepper (1986)
- *A Child's Christmas in Wales* by Dylan Thomas (1955)
- *Oxford Book of Christmas Poems* ed. Michael Harrison and Christopher Stuart-Clark (1983)
- *A Christmas Carol* by Charles Dickens (1843)
- *Little Women* by Louisa M Alcott (1869)
- *Silent Snow, Secret Snow* by Adele Geras (2003)
- *The Family from One End Street and Some Of Their Adventures* by Eve Garnett (1937)
- *Goodnight Mr Tom* by Michelle Magorian (1981)
- *The Wind in the Willows* by Kenneth Grahame (1908)

And if you've done all that ...

- Thomas Hardy took the title *Under the Greenwood Tree* from a poem by William Blake. Another of his novels *Far From the Madding Crowd* takes its title from the poem 'Elegy Written in a Country Churchyard' by Thomas Gray. Writers often 'borrow' their titles from other writers. Find out who wrote the following and where each title comes from: *Brave New World*, *Things Fall Apart*, *Murder Most Foul*, *Devices and Desires*, *Of Mice and Men*.

- How many more examples can you add to the list? Consider film and music titles too.

- In Betjeman's poem, 'Hooker's Green' and 'Crimson Lake' are not places, they are artists' colours. Other glamorous-sounding colours include Prussian blue, vermilion, yellow ochre, carmine red and ultramarine. Invent as many original names for colours as you can. Then you could make them into a colour poem. (You could also use the ones listed here.)

- John Betjeman was Poet Laureate. Find out what this means. Who is the current Poet Laureate? Prepare a short talk for the rest of your class about the office of Poet Laureate and its history.

- Find a copy of the Christmas poem 'Reindeer Report' by U A Fanthorpe. Discuss it with a friend and then perform the poem to the rest of the class.

Chapter 5 Love

'Everybody's married some time'

Silas Marner, then a lonely weaver, adopted Eppie when she was eighteen months old because her mother had collapsed and died in the snow near his cottage.

1 'Father,' said Eppie very gently, after they had been sitting in silence a little while. 'If I was to be married, ought I to be married with my mother's ring?'

Silas gave an almost imperceptible start, though the question fell in with the under-current of thought in his own mind, and then, in a subdued tone,
5 'Why, Eppie, have you been a-thinking on it?'

'Only this last week, Father,' said Eppie ingenuously, 'since Aaron talked to me about it.'

'And what did he say?' said Silas, still in the same subdued way as if he were anxious lest he should fall into the slightest tone that was not for Eppie's
10 good.

'He said he should like to be married, because he's a-going in four-and-twenty, and had got a deal of gardening work, now Mr Mott's given up. And he goes twice a week regular to Mr Cass's, and once to Mr Osgood's, and they're going to take him on at the Rectory.'

15 'And who is it as he's wanting to marry?' said Silas with rather a sad smile.

'Why, me to be sure, Daddy,' said Eppie, with dimpling laughter, kissing her father's cheek, 'as if he'd want to marry anybody else!'

'And you mean to have him, do you?' said Silas.

'Yes, some time,' said Eppie, 'I don't know when. "Everybody's married some
20 time," Aaron says. But I told him that wasn't true: For I said, "Look at Father. He's never been married."'

'No child,' said Silas, 'your father was a lone man till you was sent to him.'

'But you'll never be lone again, Father,' said Eppie tenderly. 'That was what Aaron said – "I could never think o' taking you away from Master Marner,
25 Eppie." And I said, "It 'ud be no good if you did, Aaron." And he wants us all to live together, so as you needn't work a bit, Father, only what's for your own pleasure. And he'd be as good as son to you – that was what he said.'

'And should you like that, Eppie?' said Silas, looking at her.

'I shouldn't mind it, Father,' said Eppie, quite simply. 'And I should like things
30   to be so as you needn't work much. But if it wasn't for that, I'd sooner
things didn't change. I'm very happy: I like Aaron to be fond of me and come
and see us often, and behave pretty to you – he always does behave pretty
to you, doesn't he, Father?'

'Yes, child, nobody could behave better,' said Silas, emphatically. 'He's his
35   mother's lad.'

'But I don't want any change,' said Eppie. 'I should like to go on a long, long
while just as we are. Only Aaron does want a change; and he made me cry a
bit – only a bit – because he said I didn't care for him. For if I cared for
him I should want us to be married, as he did.'

40   'Eh my blessed child,' said Silas, laying down his
pipe as if it were useless to pretend to smoke
any longer, 'you're o'er young
to be married.
We'll ask Mrs
45   Winthrop –
we'll ask Aaron's
mother what *she*
thinks: if there's a
right thing to do, she'll
50   come at it. But
there's this to be
thought on, Eppie.
Things *will*
change, whether
55   we like it or not.
Things won't go
on as they are for
a long while just as
they are and no
60   difference. I shall
get old and more
helpless and be a
burden on you
perhaps, if I don't go away from

65 you altogether. Not as I mean you'd think me a burden – I know you wouldn't – but it 'ud be hard upon you: and when I look for'ard to that, I like to think as you'd have somebody else besides me – somebody young and strong, as'll outlast your own life and take care on you to the end.' Silas paused, and resting his wrists on his knees, lifted his hands up and down
70 meditatively as he looked on the ground.

'Then would you like me to be married, Father,' said Eppie, with a little trembling in her voice.

'I'll not be the man to say no, Eppie,' said Silas emphatically. 'But we'll ask your godmother. She'll wish the right thing by you and her son too.'

From *Silas Marner* by George Eliot (1861)

EXERCISE 5.1

Answer these questions as fully as you can:

1. Explain the meaning of: (a) imperceptible (line 3), (b) subdued (line 4), (c) outlast (line 68).

2. What is Aaron's family name?

3. Summarise everything you learn from this passage about (a) Aaron and (b) his mother.

4. Referring closely to the passage, explain in your own words what Silas feels about Eppie's proposed marriage.

5. Why hasn't Eppie accepted Aaron's proposal?

6. Write three sentences of your own using the adverbs (a) ingenuously (line 6), (b) emphatically (line 73) and (c) meditatively (line 70) to show that you understand their meaning.

St Valentine

St Valentine is the patron saint of lovers. He died around 269 AD.

1   There are in fact two Valentines, whose feasts are both celebrated on 14th February in the Roman martyrology[1], neither of whom has any obvious connection with loving couples.

   The first was a Roman priest and doctor who is believed to have been
5   martyred under Claudius II on the Flaminian Way where a basilica was erected in his honour in 350 AD.

   The other was a bishop of Turni (about 60 miles from Rome) who was brought to Rome, then tortured and executed there in about 272 AD, at the command of Placidus, the ruling prefect.

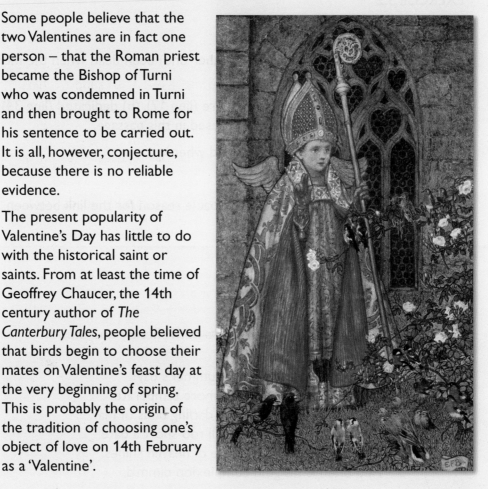

10   Some people believe that the two Valentines are in fact one person – that the Roman priest became the Bishop of Turni who was condemned in Turni
15   and then brought to Rome for his sentence to be carried out. It is all, however, conjecture, because there is no reliable evidence.

20   The present popularity of Valentine's Day has little to do with the historical saint or saints. From at least the time of Geoffrey Chaucer, the 14th
25   century author of *The Canterbury Tales*, people believed that birds begin to choose their mates on Valentine's feast day at the very beginning of spring.
30   This is probably the origin of the tradition of choosing one's object of love on 14th February as a 'Valentine'.

No British church is thought ever to have been dedicated to St Valentine,
35 but he is often represented in art with a disabled or epileptic child at his
feet whom he is thought to have cured. Other depictions show him being
beheaded for refusing to worship idols, which is what led to his martyrdom.

As well as being associated with lovers, Valentine is also the patron saint of
bee-keepers, travellers, the young and sufferers from epilepsy, fainting and
40 plague.

Notes:
[1] List of martyrs. A martyr is someone who dies for his or her beliefs.

Adapted from *The Wordsworth Dictionary of Saints* by Alison Jones (1992)

EXERCISE 5.2

Now answer these questions:

1. Roughly how long had Valentine (either one) been dead when the memorial
    was erected in the Flaminian Way?

2. Give another word for (a) conjecture (line 17), (b) dedicated (line 34),
    (c) depictions (line 36) as they are used in this passage.

3. Who wrote *The Canterbury Tales* and when?

4. Where is Turni?

5. Explain in your own words the probable reason for the link between
    14th February and lovers.

'Sonnet 18'

Read this poem carefully several times both silently and aloud:

1   Shall I compare thee to a summer's day?
        Thou art more lovely and more temperate:
        Rough winds do shake the darling buds of May,
        And summer's lease hath all too short a date:
5   Sometimes too hot the eye of heaven shines,
        And often is his gold complexion dimm'd,

And every fair from fair sometime declines,
By chance, or nature's changing course untrimm'd;
But thy eternal summer shall not fade,

10 Nor lose possession of that fair thou ow'st,
Nor shall death brag thou wander'st in his shade,
When in eternal lines to time thou grow'st;
    So long as men can breathe, or eyes can see,
    So long lives this, and this gives life to thee.

William Shakespeare (1609)

Poetry technique: metre

Poetry can be seen as notes and spaces which come together to make a 'tune' in exactly the same way as music does. In music, different time signatures give you different sorts of melody, such as a march, a waltz or a hornpipe.

In a similar way different arrangements of **metre**, as it is called in poetry, give you different sorts of poem.

Shakespeare's sonnet has five feet (the equivalent of bars in music) in each line:

So long / as men / can breathe / or eyes / can see

So long / lives this / and this / gives life / to thee

A line of poetry with five feet is called a **pentameter**. (Compare the word **pent**ameter with **pent**agon, **pent**athlon, and the delightful word **Pent**ateuch – which means the first five books in the Bible.)

Say the last two lines of Shakespeare's sonnet aloud several times. Listen to where you are putting the stresses or accents:

> So **long** / as **men** / can **breathe** / or **eyes** / can **see**
>
> So **long** / lives **this** / and **this** / gives **life** / to **thee**

Two syllables in which the first is a light 'upbeat' (unstressed) and the second a heavier syllable emphasised (stressed) by the speaker are together known as an **iamb**.

Say 'by chance' and 'but thy' aloud and listen to where your voice falls. Words like 'hello', 'mistake' and 'suppose' are iambs too.

Because Shakespeare uses iambs and pentameters, we say that this sonnet (just as many poems and plays in English, including the text of Shakespeare's plays) is written in **iambic pentameters**. That is its metre.

Iambic pentameters tend to flow very easily because they are close to the natural rhythms of spoken English:

> I left my brolly on the northern line.
>
> Are you and I to meet for tea today?
>
> Sit down and drink some lemon squash at once.

These pretty ordinary sentences are perfect examples of iambic pentameters. Try making up some of your own.

EXERCISE 5.3

Now answer the following questions. Use short quotations from the poem in your answers:

1. To whom do you think the poet is speaking?

2. Summarise what he is saying to her.

3. What is (a) 'the eye of heaven' (line 5) and (b) 'thy eternal summer' (line 9)?

4. Explain the meaning of 'And summer's lease hath all too short a date' (line 4).

5. Look carefully at the rhyme pattern of this sonnet. Why do you think Shakespeare rhymes 'shines' with 'declines' (lines 5 and 7) and 'fade' with 'shade' (lines 9 and 11)?

6. What is the meaning of the last rhyming couplet (the last two lines)?

Your turn to write

EXERCISE 5.4

1.   Write a description of the atmosphere in your school on Valentine's Day.

2.   Write a story about people falling in love with other people, with things, places or with anything you wish.

3.   Write a conversation between a mother and son about the girl he loves and their future. This could be Mrs Winthrop and Aaron from *Silas Marner*, if you wish. Look back at 'Writing workshop' in Chapters 3 and 4. Decide whether to set this out as a fictional dialogue or a playlet.

4.   Write in any way you like, taking either 'The Darling Buds of May' or 'Eternal Lines to Time' as your title.

5.   Write the story of St Valentine as colourfully as you can. Use your imagination to fill in the details.

6.   Write a poem addressed to something or someone you love.

7.   Write a story about, or a factual account of, someone in the present day suffering (or dying) for his or her beliefs.

Writing workshop

Writing a factual account

The purpose of the passage in this chapter about St Valentine is to give accurate information in a neutral way and as clearly as possible. It:

●   does not express any opinion

●   includes names and dates

●   is expressed logically in short paragraphs, moving from one point to the next

●   makes it clear (by using words and phrases such as 'conjecture', 'no reliable evidence', 'probably' and 'is thought') when the information is indisputable fact and when it is not

●   has been carefully researched.

When you write a factual account:

- Research your subject carefully using several sources.
- Make notes in your own words.
- Work out – by making a rough plan with numbered points – how you are going to present your material.
- Write your account and be sure to keep your language neutral (look back to Exercise 4.2 to be reminded of how biased language can be).
- Keep your paragraphs concise.
- Remember that, in general, short sentences are clearer than long, complicated ones.
- Similarly, in factual writing, short words are usually better than long ones so, for example, use 'start' (not 'commence'), 'buy' (not 'purchase) and 'finish' (not 'conclude').
- Edit your own work very thoroughly. Cut out any words which are unnecessary or which could be replaced by something clearer.

EXERCISE 5.5

Choose a saint – a well known one such as St George or St Paul, or a lesser known one such as St Apollonia or St Dunstan – and research him or her. Then write a short factual account of his or her life and influence. Be as accurate as you can and make your language and expression as clear as possible.

Grammar and punctuation

Phrasal verbs

Aaron usually **turns up** (arrives) at Silas and Eppie's cottage on Sunday afternoons.

Mr Jarvis **stood down** (resigned) from the committee.

We all **look up to** (admire) Shakespeare.

May I **get down** (descend) from the table?

These are examples of **phrasal verbs**. A specific **verb** and a particular **preposition** have come together and acquired a new meaning. There is almost always an alternative single word (shown in brackets in the sentences above). Overall though, we use phrasal verbs a great deal in everyday English because the alternative often seems too stilted and formal, especially in conversation.

Many phrasal verbs have acquired new meanings in addition to their original ones:

>She **turned down** the bedcovers before getting into bed.

>Miss Lang **turned down** the job offer.

>We always **stand up** when the headmaster comes in.

>I had to **stand up** for my friend because he was in trouble.

Although first language English speakers learn phrasal verbs quite easily as they grow up, non-native speakers usually find them difficult.

EXERCISE 5.6

Consider the meaning of the following phrasal verbs and use them to write some sentences of your own:

sit down	sit up	sit back	sit out	sit at
ask out	ask around	ask in	ask after	ask over
take in	take out	take up	take to	take over

EXERCISE 5.7

Supply a more formal or more direct word for the phrasal verbs used in these sentences:

1. I felt my father **pull back** when he saw the slow lorry in front.
2. Amy wants to **give up** French.
3. Jonathan decided to **put in** for the position of Head Boy.
4. The angry doctor **walked out** of the meeting.
5. We'll sing hymn number 214 but we will **leave out** the third verse.
6. The captain had to ask one of the reserves to **stand in** at the last moment.

Apostrophes

Remember that there are two uses of the **apostrophe**:

- it replaces missing letters: wouldn't, isn't, o'clock, it's (meaning 'it is' or 'it has'), S'hampton

- it shows possession: one boy's pen (singular); all the girls' hockey sticks (plural).

Note that, where a noun ends in 's', the 's' after the apostrophe is sometimes omitted. For example, one sees both 'Jesus's name' and 'Jesus' name'.

EXERCISE 5.8

Write the following sentences, adding the correct apostrophes:

1. Theyve reached home earlier than wed expected.

2. Freds cat and Mauras dog seemed to be making friends.

3. Ive just finished reading George Eliots *Adam Bede* and shall now begin Wilkie Collinss *The Woman in White*.

4. My three school dresses are all too small so were going to put them away in my younger sisters wardrobe.

5. *Lovers Vows* is the name of an old play which features in Jane Austens *Mansfield Park*.

6. Boys names and girls names are listed in the back of my grannys dictionary.

Spell check: -y adjectives becoming -ness nouns

Adjectives which end in '-y' change the 'y' to 'i' when they take the suffix 'ness', provided that the letter before the '-y' is a **consonant** (as it usually is). So:

pretty	prett**iness**
steady	stead**iness**
happy	happ**iness**
weary	wear**iness**

An adjective such as 'grey' which has a **vowel** before the '-y' simply adds 'ness' to make 'greyness'.

EXERCISE 5.9

List as many '-y' adjectives as you can; then write the correctly spelt noun ending in -ness next to each.

EXERCISE 5.10

Make sure that you can spell the following ten words taken from the passages in this chapter:

anxious	useless	laughter	possession	connection
executed	condemned	beginning	associated	martyr

Vocabulary

-dom and -hood words

The word 'martyr' is a **noun**.

As so often in English, several other words (such as 'martyrology') have developed from it.

'To martyr' is a **transitive verb** (one which requires an object to complete it). For example:

> Placidus made the decision to **martyr** Valentine.

> The English army **martyred** Joan of Arc.

'Martyrdom' is another noun meaning 'the state of being martyred'. Compare it with 'freedom' ('the state of being free') or 'wisdom' ('the state of being wise'). The suffix '-dom' has found its way into more modern words too, such as 'stardom' and 'officialdom'.

Joan of Arc was burned at the stake following a trial in which she was found guilty of heresy

Another suffix often added to words in English to mean a group of people or condition or quality is -hood.

EXERCISE 5.11

Use the following -hood words in sentences of your own:

1. falsehood
2. livelihood
3. brotherhood
4. widowhood
5. likelihood
6. priesthood
7. neighbourhood
8. knighthood

Out-, over- and under- words

'Outlast' is an example of a new word which was formed in the past from an **adverb** or **preposition** and a **verb**. It probably once had a hyphen. Today it is a single word. 'Outclass', 'outgrow', 'outdate', 'outbid' and 'outdo' are other examples. Sometimes such words then turn into **nouns** such as 'outcast' and 'outcome'. Language never stands still!

EXERCISE 5.12

List as many verbs as you can which begin with the prefixes over- and under-.

Speaking and listening

1. Work with a partner. One of you should be Silas and the other Eppie. Rehearse their conversation as it is written in the above extract. The characters should – Silas in particular – have rural Midlands accents, if you can manage them!

2. Learn by heart 'Sonnet 18' – one of the most beautiful and famous poems in English. Recite it as warmly as you can for a group or for the rest of the class.

3. Organise a small group discussion about Valentine's Day. Is it just a way for greetings card and gift manufacturers to make money, or does it have real meaning? Share your group's views with the rest of the class.

4. Prepare an individual talk about a saint, other than Valentine and the one you used for Exercise 5.5. Use a dictionary of saints or the internet. There are some remarkable ones to choose from. You might then be able to use this for a school assembly.

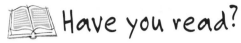 # Have you read?

The following books – some of them very famous – all have some kind of love interest. Please don't assume that this makes them 'girls' books' because they most definitely are *not*!

- *Silas Marner* by George Eliot (1861)
- *Gone With the Wind* by Margaret Mitchell (1936)
- *Pride and Prejudice* by Jane Austen (1813)
- *Saving Rafael* by Leslie Wilson (2009)
- *A Town Like Alice* by Nevil Shute (1950)
- *Tristan and Iseult* by Rosemary Sutcliff (1971)
- *Junk* by Melvyn Burgess (1996)
- *Rebecca* by Daphne du Maurier (1938)
- *You Against Me* by Jenny Downham (2010)
- *Postcards From No Man's Land* by Aidan Chambers (2001)
- *The Shell House* by Linda Newbery (2002)
- *Wuthering Heights* by Emily Brontë (1847)

✔ And if you've done all that ...

- As we learnt on page 85, **phrasal verbs** are verbs which – with a specific adverb and/or preposition – have taken on a new meaning. 'Put up with' means 'tolerate' and 'put off' means 'postpone'; 'stand up for' means 'support'; 'turn down' means 'reject' but 'turn up' means 'arrive'. List as many examples as you can. Start with 'run' (in, up, down, etc). Other everyday root verbs are 'take' and 'push,' but there are many more. Make sure you know what they mean. Some (think about 'take off') have more than one meaning.

- Use the internet or reference books to find out about the following famous pairs of lovers: Darby and Joan, Dido and Aeneas, Bonnie and Clyde, Antony and Cleopatra, Dante and Beatrice, Victoria and Albert. Make a 'Famous Couples' display area in your classroom. There are many others you could add.

- One of the most famous pieces of 'love music' ever written is Richard Wagner's 'Liebestod', part of his opera *Tristan und Isolde* (written 1857–59). It 'describes' the tragic moment when the lovers are finally separated. Borrow it from a music library or ask the school music department for a copy. Listen to it carefully several times and work out for yourself how successful you think it is.

Chapter 6 Growing up

Alexandra Rose Day

Grace Williams, the narrator of this novel, is physically very disabled. She has cerebral palsy and paralysis after having polio when she was six. She is labelled 'ineducable' and permanently confined to a mental hospital although she is not mentally impaired in any way.

1   My new built-up shoes were ready and waiting. My new built-up shoes were a surprise for Daniel. Will's suggestion.

The industrial units that had sprung up to replace the old workshops did make space for Will's cobbler's tools and equipment but they were
5   relegated to a small corner of the grand new leather-works section, where Will Sharpe was to oversee the making of a range of leather belts for a nationwide retailer. From now on, Daniel explained, most of us were going to be fitted with plastic shoes that had rubber soles glued to them.

'Cheaper,' said Daniel. 'Cheapskate', says Will. 'From a manufacturer in
10   Peterborough. And when they wear out, we'll throw them away and get a new pair, not bother sending them for mending anymore.'

Daniel was right and over the next few months the hospital became much quieter as plastic and rubber replaced leather, and muffled padding or heavy flapping replaced the echoing tap-slip-shuffle of steel and leather on lino,
15   stone, rough deal and smooth slippery, polished wood.

I was one of the people unsuitable for such shoes. I was measured for them along with everyone else, lining up in the refectory, putting my socked feet, one after the other on the flat metal plate of measuring slide, waiting while the small stranger from Peterborough nervously buckled the strap and slid
20   the measuring nut into place. I had to walk to the door of the refectory and back while the Peterborough man watched and wrote things down in a little red notebook.

Not being suitable for rubber-soled shoes, I was sent to Will Sharpe in the industrial units. My short leg had got shorter, and I was walking more and
25   more bent. But the stout pair of built-ups – one thicker than the other that Will had managed to make for me – put an end to the bends. I wasn't upright, and my hump made me hunch, but once I got the hang of the built-ups, I swanned.

30　All through May and June, I practised walking in my new shoes, with Will helping me, him clopping, me clopying, across the bare concrete floors of the half-finished industrial units. Will taught me how to turn, how to stop and even how to kick a football. He called my kick the Williams' welly and showed me pictures in his sports' pages of penalties, goals and corners, teams, flags and supporters. Spurs, Wolves, Burnley and Liverpool, Watford,
35　Pompey and the Cobblers. I became a great fan.

I was to wear my shoes for the first time on 26 June, 1962 – Alexandra Rose Day. I was ready. Mother and Father couldn't attend the celebrations that year, but I scarcely cared. I was fifteen. My heart was beating.

Alexandra Rose Day dawned pink and full of promise. The nurses rushed, as
40　keen as us. We were taken for breakfast to the main refectory in our nightgowns and barefoot, so that the whole ward could be stripped and tidied earlier than usual.

There were too many people in the refectory, too many grown-up men and women. There was joshing and pushing. When it was time to carry our
45　plates to the end of the room for washing, the joshing and pushing got worse. A man, wearing boots, stood on my bare toe. I tripped and swore.

I knocked into a nurse I'd never seen before. She started shouting,
50　first at me and then at Nurse Halliday who was new and young. Nurse Halliday looked to Nurse Hughes for
55　help, but Nurse Hughes was busy with Ida, who was trying to steal slices of wet bread from the slop
60　bucket.

Nurse Halliday said I'd have to be punished.

From *Grace Williams Says It Loud* by Emma Henderson (2010)

EXERCISE 6.1

Answer the following questions as fully as you can:

1. Why is Grace so excited about her new shoes?

2. What is Will Sharpe's role in the hospital?

3. In which year was Grace born?

4. Summarise what you deduce about Grace's disability from this passage.

5. What does the word 'clopying' tell you about Grace's personality?

6. Describe in your own words the incident which led to Grace being told she would be punished.

7. What form do you think the punishment took?

Life in a Liberty Bodice

In this extract from an autobiography, the author describes growing up in the 1920s.

1   For most of 1924 I was 14, the awkward age when dreams of what one might be are light years away from what one is. Like many adolescents of that and this period, I was awkward and shy with those who were unfamiliar but impudent and pert with those I knew well. But not with parents and
5   their friends; it was a heinous sin 'to answer back.' Elders were always assumed – often inaccurately – to be our betters whom we had, without reasoning, to respect.

My mother had brought us up to be clean and plain. Not in so many words, but she made it quite clear that beauty was elsewhere. She had no feminine
10   penchant for dressing up, making up or making up to men although she looked engagingly feminine herself. Beauty, as far as my mother was concerned, was quite distant from her daughters and I cannot remember any of us having one feature or talent praised. Beauty, in my mother's book, was something caught on the brush by a Burne-Jones, a Watts or a Rossetti
15   and their limpid ladies were certainly not for man-handling.

Unlike the Pre-Raphaelite ladies with their loose girdles and their close-fitting morals, our English rose skins were too often blemished with a

blackhead or a spot, a condition which evoked no sympathy from my
mother who loftily assumed that it was a lack of washing. It was a lonely
20 and nerve-wracking business, nose against the mirror, going into battle
against any guilty pore and then trying to disguise it with an unhygienic dab
from a secret powder compact.

So we grew up through those threshold years with a Kiplingesque idea that
a schoolgirl's role and goal was to be a man, my son! How romance ever
25 insinuated its way into our lives was
to be marvelled at. But in a naïve way
it did.

My mother, as I have already told, had
a genius for attracting into our home
30 people who shared high-minded
thoughts, words and music. Regular
visitors were George Wilkinson, a
magnetic lecturer in English at the
training College in Leeds, and our
35 oldest cousin Austin, a superb
raconteur of North and East Riding
dialect, and, at that time, Second
Master at Woodhouse Grove School.

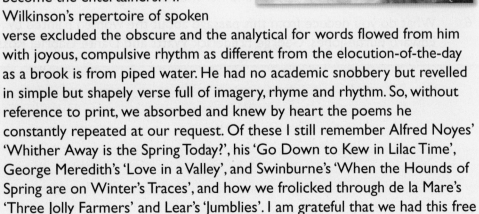

Throughout our childhood, our home
40 vibrated with do-it-yourself
entertainment, and we children – a
captive audience – needed no
persuading to change roles and
become the entertainers. Mr
45 Wilkinson's repertoire of spoken
verse excluded the obscure and the analytical for words flowed from him
with joyous, compulsive rhythm as different from the elocution-of-the-day
as a brook is from piped water. He had no academic snobbery but revelled
in simple but shapely verse full of imagery, rhyme and rhythm. So, without
50 reference to print, we absorbed and knew by heart the poems he
constantly repeated at our request. Of these I still remember Alfred Noyes'
'Whither Away is the Spring Today?', his 'Go Down to Kew in Lilac Time',
George Meredith's 'Love in a Valley', and Swinburne's 'When the Hounds of
Spring are on Winter's Traces', and how we frolicked through de la Mare's
55 'Three Jolly Farmers' and Lear's 'Jumblies'. I am grateful that we had this free

ride before being caught in the grip of modern intellectual poets whose stark prosaic lines took much of the joy and the music out of verse-speaking.

60   We girls sparkled and responded to George Wilkinson – a charmer – but as he was married and middle-aged, he was reserved for relaxed hero-worshipping. The next best thing, as far as I was concerned, was his son, Peter, who though not as verbally romantic as his father, was accessible and approved of by my mother and cousin Austin. Fortuitously for me he was also at Woodhouse Grove, a sixth form boarder, so it was easy to arrange a
65   family visit of the Hydes and Mr Wilkinson to Woodhouse Grove with Austin as our host. My heart soared with the idea of Sunday tea and evening service at a boys' boarding school – his school.

From *Life in a Liberty Bodice* by Christabel Burniston (1991)

EXERCISE 6.2

Answer these questions as fully as you can:

1.   Find single words in the passage which mean (a) impolite, (b) story teller, (c) bare, (d) passion.

2.   How old was Christabel Burniston when the new edition of her book was published?

3.   Explain what the author means by a 'free ride' (lines 55–56).

4.   Summarise what the author liked about George Wilkinson.

5.   In which ways did the author and her mother disagree?

6.   What do you deduce from this passage about the women painted by Edward Burne-Jones, George Frederick Watts and Dante Gabriel Rossetti?

'Timothy Winters'

Read this poem several times both silently and aloud:

1
    Timothy Winters comes to school
    With eyes as wide as a football pool,
    Ears like bombs and teeth like splinters:
    A blitz of a boy is Timothy Winters.

5
    His belly is white, his neck is dark,
    And his hair is an exclamation mark,
    His clothes are enough to scare a crow
    And through his britches the blue winds blow.

    When teacher talks he won't hear a word
10
    And he shoots down dead the arithmetic-bird,
    He licks the patterns off his plate
    And he's not even heard of the Welfare State.

    Timothy Winters has bloody feet
    And he lives in a house on Suez Street,
15
    He sleeps in a sack on the kitchen floor
    And they say there aren't boys like him any more.

                    Old Man Winters likes his beer
                    And his missus ran off with a bombardier,
                    Grandma sits in the grate with a gin
20   And Timothy's dosed with aspirin.

                    The Welfare Worker lies awake
                    But the law's as tricky as a ten-foot snake,
                    So Timothy Winters drinks his cup
                    And slowly goes on growing up.

25   At Morning Prayers the Master helves[1]
                    For children less fortunate than ourselves,
                    And the loudest response in the room is when
                    Timothy Winters roars 'Amen!'

                    So come one angel, come on ten:
30   Timothy Winters says 'Amen
                    Amen amen amen amen.'
                    Timothy Winters, Lord.

                    Amen

                    Charles Causley

                    Notes:
                    [1] Prays

Poetry technique: symbolism

A **symbol** is an object which represents something much bigger and more important than itself. For example, although the Union Flag is literally just a piece of flapping, coloured fabric, it stands for Great Britain. It is a symbol of Britain. In the same way, a wedding ring is really only a small hoop of metal but it stands for, and is a symbol of, a marriage.

Poets and other writers often use symbolism to represent abstract ideas. In 'Timothy Winters' the 'sack on the kitchen floor' is a symbol of his poverty. In 'Sonnet 18' 'the darling buds of May' symbolise youthful beauty and in 'Circus Lion' the bars represent the lions' loss of freedom.

Read through all the poems we have looked at so far in this book for other examples of symbolism.

EXERCISE 6.3

Answer these questions about Charles Causley's poem:

1. What aspects of Timothy's appearance suggest that there are problems at home?

2. Describe his family.

3. What is meant by 'the law's as tricky as a ten-foot snake' (line 22)?

4. Explain in your own words what you think Charles Causley means by the last verse.

5. What does the rhyme and rhythm in this poem add to your understanding of it?

6. (a) What does the poet mean by 'shoots down dead the arithmetic-bird' (line 10)?

   (b) Why does he put it like this?

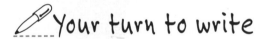 Your turn to write

EXERCISE 6.4

1. Write a story about a disabled child.

2. Write a news item for a newspaper about a sporting or educational achievement by a disabled child.

3. Write about a family friend or other regular visitor to your home.

4. Write a poem about anything you like, modelled on 'Timothy Winters' and with a verse pattern and rhymes similar to those used by Charles Causley. You might start, for instance, 'Jessica Smithers comes to town with jeans as loose as a dressing gown …'

5. Write about growing up in any way you wish.

6. Is it harder to grow up in the 21st century than it was when your parents or grandparents were your age? Write your views.

Writing workshop

Life writing

Although it reads like a personal account *Grace Williams Says It Loud* is fiction. *Life in a Liberty Bodice*, however, is Christabel Burniston's autobiography – or account of her life – an example of what is sometimes now called 'life writing'.

Life writing can include:

- biography
- autobiography
- memoirs
- articles based on personal experience
- diaries
- letters
- blogs
- emails
- anything which requires the writer, or person he or she is writing about, to look back and remember.

Make life writing lively by:

- focusing on vivid details – such as Christabel Burniston trying to disguise her spots behind her mother's back
- choosing vocabulary with precision (as in all your writing) – such as Christabel Burniston's use of 'threshold', 'magnetic' and 'soared'
- sometimes looking back from the present and commenting on the past – Christabel Burniston remarks that she still knows some of the poems she learnt in her early teens and compares being a teenager in the 1920s with the 1990s
- remembering that it's usually how you tell it rather than what you're writing about which makes life writing interesting and successful.

EXERCISE 6.5

Think of something which happened to you or to, or in, your family at some point in the past. It could be:

- something very significant such as your having an accident or the death of a relative

- something quite ordinary such as the visit to your home of some relatives that you don't often see

- your first day at school, the birth of a younger brother or sister

- anything else at all.

Make notes on your memories – trying to find words and phrases which are particularly apt.

Build your notes into a short piece of polished life writing.

Grammar and punctuation

Sentences

There are three sorts of sentence.

1. These are **simple** sentences:

    He slept.   She was the elder.

    In a simple sentence, there is one subject, one verb and it makes a single statement.

    In grammar this is its precise meaning and it does not mean, for example, that a simple idea is being expressed.

2. This is a **compound** sentence:

    He had no academic snobbery but revelled in simple but shapely verse, full of imagery, rhyme and rhythm.

    It makes two equally weighted statements: (i) 'He had no academic snobbery' and (ii) 'He revelled in simple but shapely verse, full of imagery, rhyme and rhythm'.

    The statements are hooked together with the conjunction 'but'.

    A compound sentence is one in which two or more statements are joined with conjunctions. Here is another example:

    Mother couldn't attend the celebrations that year but I scarcely cared.

3.   This is a **complex** sentence:

> My mother, as I have already told, had a genius for attracting into our home people who shared high-minded thoughts, words and music.

The main statement is: 'My mother had a genius for attracting people into our home'.

'As I have already told' and 'who shared high-minded thought, words and music' give extra information. They are groups of words – known as clauses – which act like adverbs and adjectives. They are called **subordinate clauses** because they are secondary to the sentence's main statement.

'As I have already told' is an **adverbial clause** because it adds to the meaning of (or qualifies or modifies) the main verb 'had'.

'Who shared high-minded thoughts, words and music' is an **adjectival clause** because it adds to the meaning of (or qualifies or modifies) the word 'people'.

EXERCISE 6.6

Which of the types of sentence described above is each of the following?

1.   Charles, who loves cricket and football, has broken his leg.

2.   Maisie ran for help and Jamila looked after their sick friend.

3.   I adore chocolate, spaghetti, avocados and apple crumble.

4.   One twin is tall but the other is quite short.

5.   Our school, which was badly flooded during the holidays, cannot now open on time.

6.   She laughed.

7.   My sister, as you know, is very keen on disco dancing which she does on Tuesdays at a club in town.

8.   Paul cooked the meal but everyone helped him clear up.

EXERCISE 6.7

Build each of the following simple sentences into a compound one by adding other statements joined with conjunctions:

1. I cried.

2. My mother was furious.

3. We were eating ice cream.

4. Max is running.

5. Let's ask Rina.

EXERCISE 6.8

Build each of the simple sentences in Exercise 6.7 into complex ones by adding adjectival and adverbial clauses.

Spell check: words/phrases starting al- or all

If 'all' is used as prefix, it has only one 'l'. So:

already   **al**though   **al**ways   **al**most   **al**together

Interestingly, each of these can also be used as two words, although the meaning and the grammar is different. For example:

Are we **all ready** for school? ('All' is an adverb and 'ready' is an adjective.)

Is it six o'clock **already**? ('Already' is an adverb.)

That is why it's particularly important to spell these correctly because – in this case – spelling affects meaning.

EXERCISE 6.9

Make up sentences using these pairs. Write one sentence for each (eight in total):

1. all though   although
2. all ways   always
3. all most   almost
4. all together   altogether

Learn: 'all right' is two words in formal writing but informally can be spelt 'alright'.

EXERCISE 6.10

Learn the spelling of the following ten words all taken from the passages above:

measuring	paralysis	echoing	practised	equipment
adolescents	unhygienic	naïve	accessible	arithmetic

Vocabulary

Words from Greek and Latin deities

'Hygiene' comes from the name of the Greek goddess of health, *Hygeia*.

Many English words derive from Greek and Latin gods and goddesses, or from notable figures in mythology.

A statue of the Greek titan Atlas which shows him supporting the Earth on his shoulders

EXERCISE 6.11

Look up the following words in a good dictionary and make a note of their meanings (if you don't know them) and origins:

1. cereal
2. mercurial
3. jovial
4. venerate
5. vulcanise

6. martial
7. hypnotic
8. tantalise
9. herculean
10. floral

-arian words

Sometimes a person gets a noun ending in -arian attached to him or her because of job, role, status or attitude.

For example, Christabel Burniston was a **nonagenarian** when she died. She was in her nineties. A **parliamentarian** is another word for a member of parliament or MP and a **centenarian** is someone who has passed his or her 100th birthday.

EXERCISE 6.12

Write the following sentences using the correct -arian words from the list to fill in the gaps:

egalitarian   grammarian   vegetarian   librarian
antiquarian   disciplinarian

1. I found a wonderful old copy of *Oliver Twist* in an _____ bookshop.

2. The class was relieved to find its new teacher much less of a _____ than its old one.

3. Like my brother, Freddie, rabbits and rhinoceroses are _____.

4. Britain has a much more _____ system of electing its government than many developing countries.

5. Anyone who studies English from this book is well on his or her way to becoming a _____ !

6. The _____ is responsible for all the new book purchases in our school.

EXERCISE 6.13

Write sentences of your own to show you understand the meaning of:

1. septuagenarian   4. authoritarian

2. fruitarian   5. veterinarian

3. sectarian   6. agrarian

Speaking and listening

1. Read one of the books in the 'Have you read?' section. Spend two minutes trying to persuade the rest of the class to read it.

2. Interview an elderly person about his or her memories of growing up. (You could choose someone known to your family, to whom you talk out of school; alternatively, with your teacher's help, you could invite some interviewees into school.)

3. 'The hardest thing about growing up is …' Talk on this topic for one minute to a small group. Take it in turns.

4. With a partner discuss any aspect of growing up which interests you both.

 Have you read?

All these books feature young people growing up:

- *Butterfly Summer* by Anne-Marie Conway (2012)
- *Life in a Liberty Bodice* by Christabel Burniston (1991)
- *I Had A Little Cat: Collected Poems for Children* by Charles Causley (1996)
- *Sisterland* by Linda Newbery (2003)
- *Catcher in the Rye* by J D Salinger (1951)
- *A Gathering Light* by Jennifer Donnelly (2003)
- *Great Expectations* by Charles Dickens (1861)
- *The Diary of a Young Girl; Definitive Edition* by Anne Frank (1947)
- *The Garbage King* by Elizabeth Laird (2003)
- *Cider With Rosie* by Laurie Lee (1959)
- *Grace Williams Says It Loud** by Emma Henderson (2010)

- *My Dad is Ten Years Old* by Mark O'Sullivan (2011)
- *Angela's Ashes* by Frank McCourt (1996)

* Although *Grace Williams Says It Loud* is in some ways quite an adult book, if your parents and teachers are happy for you to read it, you will find it contains many insights about growing up, and about disability.

✔ And if you've done all that ...

- *Grace Williams Says It Loud* is about a child who was declared 'ineducable' – a category which no longer exists. Find out what this used to mean and what the implications were. In what ways do you think life for disabled people has improved in the last 50 years or so? If you can, talk to some older disabled people and get their views too.

- Find out everything you can about Burne-Jones, G F Watts and Dante Gabriel Rossetti, the three artists mentioned by Christabel Burniston.

- Look at this anagram star:

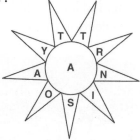

Make as many words as you can with four letters or more by rearranging the letters in the star. Every word you make must include the letter in the centre. One of your words should use all ten letters. Aim for 30 words.

Now invent anagram stars for your friends to work on. Use seven-, eight-, nine- or ten- letter words and work out the answers yourself before passing a puzzle on to anyone else.

Chapter 7 London

Sherlock Holmes tackles a murder in South London

This passage comes from the first of the long and famous series of books about the amateur detective Sherlock Holmes. The narrator – Holmes's friend Dr Watson – describes a visit to a house in South London where a murder has taken place.

1   He hustled on his overcoat, and bustled about in a way that showed that an energetic fit had superseded the apathetic one.

'Get your hat,' he said.

'You wish me to come?'

5   'Yes, if you have nothing better to do.' A minute later we were both in a hansom[1], driving furiously for the Brixton Road.

It was a foggy, cloudy morning, and a dun-coloured veil hung over the house-tops, looking like the reflection of the mud-coloured streets beneath. My

10   companion was in the best of spirits, and prattled away about Cremona fiddles, and the difference between

15   a Stradivarius and an Amati. As for myself, I was silent, for the dull weather and the melancholy business

20   upon which we were engaged depressed my spirits.

'You don't seem to give much thought to the

25   matter in hand,' I said at last, interrupting Holmes' musical disquisition.

'No data yet,' he answered. 'It is a capital mistake to theorise before you
30   have all the evidence. It biases the judgment.'

'You will have your data soon,' I remarked, pointing with my finger; 'this is
the Brixton Road, and that is the house, if I am not very much mistaken.'

'So it is. Stop, driver, stop!' We were still a hundred yards or so from it, but
he insisted upon our alighting, and we finished our journey upon foot.

35   Number 3, Lauriston Gardens wore an ill-omened and minatory look. It
was one of four which stood back some little way from the street, two
being occupied and two empty. The latter looked out with three tiers of
vacant melancholy windows, which were blank and dreary, save that here
and there a 'To Let' card had developed like a cataract upon the bleared
40   panes. A small garden sprinkled over with a scattered eruption of sickly
plants separated each of these houses from the street, and was traversed by
a narrow pathway, yellowish in colour, and consisting apparently of a
mixture of clay and of gravel. The whole place was very sloppy from the rain
which had fallen through the night. The garden was bounded by a three-foot
45   brick wall with a fringe of wood rails upon the top, and against this wall was
leaning a stalwart police constable, surrounded by a small knot of loafers,
who craned their necks and strained their eyes in the vain hope of catching
some glimpse of the proceedings within.

I had imagined that Sherlock Holmes would at once have hurried into the
50   house and plunged into a study of the mystery. Nothing appeared to be
further from his intention. With an air of nonchalance which, under the
circumstances, seemed to me to border upon affectation, he lounged up and
down the pavement, and gazed vacantly at the ground, the sky, the opposite
houses and the line of railings. Having finished his scrutiny, he proceeded
55   slowly down the path, or rather down the fringe of grass which flanked the
path, keeping his eyes riveted upon the ground. Twice he stopped, and once
I saw him smile, and heard him utter an exclamation of satisfaction. There
were many marks of footsteps upon the wet clayey soil, but since the police
had been coming and going over it, I was unable to see how my companion
60   could hope to learn anything from it. Still, I had had such extraordinary
evidence of the quickness of his perceptive faculties, that I had no doubt
that he could see a great deal which was hidden from me.

From *A Study in Scarlet* by Arthur Conan Doyle (1887)

Notes:
[1] Horse-drawn taxi-cab

EXERCISE 7.1

Answer these questions as fully as you can:

1. Explain the meaning of (a) superseded (line 2), (b) disquisition (line 28), (c) stalwart (line 46), (d) nonchalance (line 51).

2. Find single words in the passage which mean (a) close inspection, (b) an attitude of showing off, (c) crossed, (d) threatening.

3. What evidence is there in this passage that Holmes is a more intelligent man than Watson?

4. Which seven adjectives in the first three sentences of the paragraph about number 3, Lauriston Gardens make it clear that nothing happy can have happened there?

5. What does Holmes 'prattle' about on the journey (line 12) and why?

6. Which other people are present at Lauriston Gardens and what are they doing when Holmes and Watson arrive?

London's history

This passage, an example of clear non-fiction writing, explains to tourists how and why London has developed from a small Thames crossing into the vast city it is now.

1   Londinium was founded by the Romans at a convenient crossing of the Thames, though it had been convenient for the local inhabitants too. Tacitus, a Roman historian, describes a flourishing trading city existing in AD 67. The area was marshy but there was a low hill, roughly where the Bank of
5   England now stands, and it was here that the Romans chose to build a typical Roman city, primarily for military reasons. Their forum was where Leadenhall market now stands.

The Romans believed that Britain was a kind of El Dorado, and that they'd make their fortune here. The river was navigable a long way inland, and tidal,
10 which made it easy to get boats in and out.

England, at that time, was inhabited by a hodge-podge of tribes and small kingdoms, and the Romans had little difficulty subduing them – despite some noble efforts at defence. The locals assimilated Roman culture and,

15   after a couple of hundred years, were more Roman than the Romans. When the Romans pulled out, pressured by frontier wars, the Saxons took over.

They hated living in the old walled Roman city and established their own city of long huts, roughly where Covent Garden is today. This duality still persists – the 'City' is essentially Roman Londinium, and 'Westminster' is the Saxon add-on.

20   When new invaders swept the country the Saxons and their kin moved back into the safety of the old Roman City, by then quite deserted, and it was here that London originated.

By the time the Normans took over from the
25   Saxons after 1066, the basis of the mercantile capital was already laid. A charter of citizens' rights and a confederation of
30   tradesmen provided a counterweight to the aristocracy.

London was a leading trading port of western
35   Europe. Merchants from Italy, the Netherlands, France and Germany lived around the river, which had only one crossing – the Old London Bridge – until 1769. Food and wine came in. Wool and leather went out. Due to the wool trade's centre in East Anglia – near the old Boston – London was for a time England's second city. However, the establishment of merchants'
40   guilds, with the mayor at their head, re-established London's place as capital.

These medieval guilds and livery companies still exist today and preserve fine buildings across the City. The Weavers' Company dates back to 1130, the Saddlers' Company goes back to 1272, the Wax Chandlers' Company to 1358, though the Launderers' Guild was formed as late as 1960.
45   Napoleon's jibe that Britain was 'a nation of shopkeepers' is true. And, with a living to defend from invaders, and trading routes and privileges to protect overseas, it was unsurprising that they made doughty fighters – as the French learned to their cost at Crécy and Agincourt.

In Tudor times – after years wasted in wars of succession (which explains
50   Henry VIII's desperate and bloody attempts to secure a male heir) – the

Dissolution of the Monasteries and terrible religious persecutions led to poverty and mass unemployment. And the Black Death and other plagues decimated the population.

55 However, by the late 16th century, the seeds of England's future as a world trading power were sown with the formation of the Trading Companies – The East India Company, The Muscovy Company, The Levant Company and the Turkey Company. Such companies – supported by Britain's naval prowess – created new management techniques which conquered the world and are still in use today. England was also at the forefront of the arts

60 with a lively theatre and music scene.

The plague in 1665 and the fire in 1666 shook London out of its complacency, but also led to a wave of property development – which is still going on. Wren, Hawksmoor and other forerunners of Sir Richard Rogers were soon dominating the city skylines.

65 The redevelopment continued into the 18th century with buildings like The Bank of England and most of the bridges across the Thames springing up. Tower Bridge was opened in 1894. The Victorians supervised the transformation of London into a modern city with sewers and an underground railway (1863). Overground railways (1836) and omnibuses

70 (1855) crossed the city, and the port of London enjoyed a final flowering.

Despite the presence of the royal palaces, Westminster Abbey (a place of pilgrimage) and the country's first printing presses, Westminster really only came into its own in the 19th century and was granted the title of a City, with its own mayor, in 1900. Until the 1850s it was the haunt of criminals,

75 who used the sanctuary laws to hide in the precincts of Westminster Abbey. The redesigning of the area under Charles Barry put paid to this unsavoury aspect and saw an expansion which coincided with the arrival of the railways. Nearby Victoria Station occupies the site of several private railway stations which were amalgamated in 1899.

80 The two World Wars saw huge destruction, both to the people and to the city, and some unfortunate rebuilding followed, with little real conservation work. Many of the city's worst buildings date from this time, when the Greater London Council changed the face of the old city forever. It is said that the GLC did more damage to London than the Luftwaffe[1].

Abridged from www.londontourist.org

Notes:
[1] German airforce

EXERCISE 7.2

Answer these questions as fully as you can:

1. Which 19th century architect redesigned the Westminster area?

2. What did the Romans find practical about Londinium?

3. In what sense, according to this author, are the British a 'nation of shopkeepers' (line 45)?

4. What happened at Crécy and Agincourt?

5. What were England's major exports in medieval times?

6. Explain in your own words what the author means by 'the GLC did more damage to London than the Luftwaffe' (line 84).

7. Where did the idea that London is made up of two cities – Westminster and the City of London – come from?

8. Summarise the difficulties experienced by Londoners in Tudor times.

'Composed upon Westminster Bridge, September 3 1802'

1   Earth has not anything to show more fair:
     Dull would he be of soul who could pass by
     A sight so touching in its majesty:
     This city now doth, like a garment, wear
5   The beauty of the morning, silent, bare,

Ships, towers, domes, theatres and temples lie
Open unto the fields, and to the sky;
All bright and glittering in the smokeless air.
Never did sun more beautifully steep[1]
10   In his first splendour, valley, rock or hill;
Ne'r saw I, never felt, a calm so deep!
The river glideth at his own sweet will:
Dear God! the very houses seem asleep;
And all that mighty heart is lying still.

William Wordsworth (1807)

Notes:
[1] Soak

Poetry technique: personification

Personification is a specific sort of metaphor in which a comparison is made between something inanimate and a human being. When something is being compared with a person, it is **personified**.

In 'This city now doth, like a garment, wear …' Wordsworth is personifying the city by imagining it as a human being who can 'wear the beauty of the morning'.

Later in the poem he personifies first the river and then the houses too. Work out where this happens.

Compare these examples of personification with John Betjeman's treatment of London in the fourth verse of 'Christmas' and with Wole Soyinka's presentation of Voice in the seventh line of 'Telephone Conversation'.

(What is the metre of 'Composed upon Westminster Bridge'? Look at it carefully and compare it with Shakespeare's 'Sonnet 18'.)

EXERCISE 7.3

Answer these questions. Use your own words and quotations from the poem:

1. What time of day is it in Wordsworth's sonnet and how do you know?

2. Pick out four individual words which suggest that Wordsworth is enthusiastic about what he is seeing.

3. Wordsworth uses personification four times in this poem. Find these four times and say for each whether you think the description is effective and why.

4. What buildings can Wordsworth see?

5. Which phrase in the poem tells you that London was much smaller in 1802 than it is now?

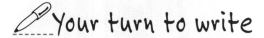 Your turn to write

EXERCISE 7.4

1. Describe a visit to London based on your own experience.

2. Write about a place in London and someone's arrival there. Make the details as sinister as you can, so that the reader knows something unpleasant is about to happen.

3. Write a poem – perhaps a sonnet shaped like Wordsworth's 'Composed upon Westminster Bridge' – about a place you know and like. It could be in London or it could be anywhere you wish.

4. Write about London or another city in any way you wish.

5. Write a leaflet advertising an attraction in London, or some other city which you know well. You can almost certainly get extra information from the internet to help you with this.

6. Write a short story in which London plays an important part.

✎ Writing workshop

Factual writing

The passage in this chapter about the history of London is an example of factual writing. It was published on a website which acts like a guidebook. Its purpose is to provide accurate information for people who want to know more about the history of the city they are visiting or planning to visit.

Notice that the piece:

- contains facts in every sentence

- is written in everyday language ('… the Saxons took over' 'Westminster really only came into its own') rather than being expressed in a very stilted or formal way

- does not, however, avoid adult words such as 'counterweight' 'decimated' and 'precincts'

- is laid out in fairly short paragraphs

- makes good use of linking words (sometimes called 'connectives') such as 'however' and 'despite' and conjunctions such as 'and' and 'but' to make the language and ideas flow

- summarises something which could be much longer and more complicated

- relates the information to the present whenever possible

- is crisp and quite entertaining to read

- could be read for information by adults or older children.

Look closely too at how the writer varies the shape of his or her sentences. Some start with the subject but many do not. Sentence length is well varied too so that there is a rhythm in the writing – try reading it aloud to feel this if you don't sense it from reading the passage silently.

There is more information and advice about how to vary sentence shape in the 'Grammar and punctuation' section in Chapter 8.

EXERCISE 7.5

Write an accurate, factual account of the history of one of these:

- a building known to you
- the city, town or village you live in
- your school
- your home.

Use books and the internet to help you assemble the information.

Keep your writing as 'tight' as you can by modelling it on the passage about London's history – including the factors in it listed above – although your writing can be shorter if you wish.

Grammar and punctuation

Voice

All verbs are expressed in either the **active voice** or the **passive voice**. Voice is quite different from tense. Whatever tense you're using, you have to use one voice or the other.

Londinium **was founded** by the Romans.	(passive)
The Romans **founded** Londinium.	(active)
It **is said** that …	(passive)
People (or 'they') **say** that …	(active)
This book **has been read** by eleven pupils.	(passive)
Eleven pupils **have read** this book.	(active)
It **will be agreed** that term will end on 20th July.	(passive)
We **shall agree** to end term on 20th July.	(active)

It is a matter of reversing the subject and object. Clearly, the writer of the first example wanted – for emphasis – to start his piece with the word 'Londinium'.

There is scope for both voices in writing but note that:

- The passive voice often needs the word 'by'. It usually uses more words and requires a more complex form of the verb.

- The active form is usually more straightforward and direct and therefore generally better.

Politicians often hide behind the passive voice with expressions like 'It has been decided that …' rather than 'We have decided …' or 'I am asked by voters …' rather than 'Voters ask me …'

The passive voice can be very evasive!

EXERCISE 7.6

Change the active voice to the passive in these sentences:

1. Before the end of the month, the architect completed the plans.
2. The hockey player hit the ball a long way with her stick.
3. Nathan made some biscuits.
4. In 1066, William of Normandy took London.
5. The motorcyclist knocked down the old lady.
6. Mrs Johnson cleared the electronic whiteboard.

EXERCISE 7.7

This passage is written in the passive voice. Notice how stilted and awkward it sounds. Change it to the active. You will have to change some words:

> The conservatory was erected by Mary Swavesey and her sisters. The site had been measured and levelled by Gail. The sections of the conservatory had been prepared by Emma. Then the conservatory was put in place by the three sisters working together. It had been ordered and paid for by Mr Newington. The sisters were praised by him for a fine piece of work.

Transitive and intransitive verbs

All verbs are transitive or intransitive.

A **transitive** verb requires an object to complete its meaning.

An **intransitive** verb makes sense without an object.

For example:

> Tacitus **describes** … This needs 'a flourishing trading city' to complete its meaning.
> Number 3, Lauriston Gardens **wore** … This needs 'an ill-omened and minatory look' to complete its meaning.

'Describe' and 'wore' are transitive verbs.

Examples of intransitive verbs:

> The river **glideth**.
> Several private railway stations **were amalgamated**.

These are complete statements. No object is required.

EXERCISE 7.8

Add objects (be inventive!) to these sentences to complete their transitive verbs:

1. The Victorians supervised …
2. Omnibuses crossed …
3. The Port of London enjoyed …
4. I asked …
5. We represented …
6. My mother saw …

Look very carefully at the punctuation in the first half of the extract from *A Study in Scarlet* at the beginning of this chapter. It is a fine example of how to set out and punctuate direct speech (see Chapter 3).

EXERCISE 7.9

Write a short conversation between two people who are either travelling through London or discussing doing so. Take great care to punctuate it accurately.

Spell check: plurals of -o nouns

Most nouns ending in '-o' in the singular take 's' in the plural.
That includes the following:

1. Words of Spanish and Italian origin and musical nouns:

poncho	ponchos
banjo	banjos
concerto	concertos
patio	patios

2. Abbreviated nouns:

photo	photos
disco	discos

3.   Nouns which end in a double vowel in the singular:

studio	studios
zoo	zoos

However, there are thirteen quite common words ending in '-o' which take 'es' in the plural. These are:

buffalo	buffalo**es**
cargo	cargo**es**
domino	domino**es**
echo	echo**es**
hero	hero**es**
memento	memento**es**
mosquito	mosquito**es**
negro	negro**es**
potato	potato**es**
tomato	tomato**es**
tornado	tornado**es**
torpedo	torpedo**es**
volcano	volcano**es**

EXERCISE 7.10

These words all take 's' when they become plural. Using a dictionary if you need to, work out which of the three categories above they fit into:

lasso	soprano
kangaroo	tattoo
scenario	hippo
embryo	biro
radio	albino

N.B. Take care with these two words: **libretto**, plural: **libretti** and **virtuoso**, plural: **virtuosi**.

A virtuoso is someone with outstanding skill in his or her discipline

EXERCISE 7.11

Learn the spelling of these ten words which are all used in the three passages above:

superseded   interrupting   developed   separated   extraordinary

assimilated   essentially   privileges   succession   techniques

Vocabulary

Words from *navis* and *ruptura*

The word 'navigable' means 'able to be negotiated' by ship or boat. It comes from the Latin word *navis*, meaning 'ship'. From it we also get 'navy', 'navigate', 'navigator', 'navigation' and the splendid word 'navicular' which means 'boat-shaped'.

An 'eruption' is an 'outbreak' from the Latin words e, meaning 'out', and *ruptura*, 'a breaking'. We get 'rupture' from the same root, along with 'interrupt' (to 'break into' something) and 'abrupt' (suddenly 'breaking away').

EXERCISE 7.12

Choose six of the above *navis* and *ruptura* words and use them in sentences of your own to make the meaning clear.

Alliterative rhyming

'Hodge-podge' means an 'assortment' or a 'jumble'. Like 'hotch-potch', it has found its way into the language because people like pairs of words which rhyme and/or alliterate (contain the same sounds).

EXERCISE 7.13

Use a good dictionary to find out the meanings and origins of these expressions:

1. namby pamby
2. hanky panky
3. wishy washy
4. willy nilly
5. shilly shally
6. niminy piminy
7. airy fairy
8. hocus pocus

Another useful reference book for research of this sort is *Brewer's Dictionary of Phrase and Fable* which you can find in most libraries.

Speaking and listening

1. Collect as many poems as you can which have something to do with London. Organise a class festival of London poetry in which you all read out and share the poems you have found.

2. Organise discussions in small groups on the topic: 'Which is best: town or country?' Make notes on your group's thoughts and prepare a notice board display with other groups in the class.

3. Take it in turns to speak for one minute each on the best thing you've ever seen or done in London. When they do this on Radio 4's quiz programme *Just a Minute*, panellists have to speak without hesitation, repetition or deviation. Try it!

 # Have you read?

London plays a major part in all these books:

- *The Sign of Four* (and other Sherlock Holmes stories) by A Conan Doyle (1897)
- *Little Soldier* by Bernard Ashley (2001)
- *The Moonstone* by Wilkie Collins (1868)
- *Coram Boy* by Jamila Gavin (2000)
- *The Keys to the Street* by Ruth Rendell (1996)
- *Girls Out Late* by Jacqueline Wilson (1999)
- *Brick Lane* by Monica Ali (2003)
- *Traitor's Kiss* by Pauline Francis (2011)
- *The Graveyard Book* by Neil Gaiman (2008)
- *Fever* by Dee Shulman (2012)

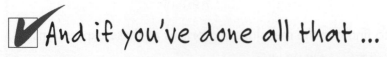 # And if you've done all that ...

- Listen to *A London Symphony* by Ralph Vaughan Williams (1913) and/or Edward Elgar's *Cockaigne Overture: In London Town* (1901). The music department in your school may be able to help. Or refer to www.bbc.co.uk/radio3

  Both pieces try to present the everyday sounds of London. Decide how well you think they work.

- Read the famous descriptions of 17th century London – especially the Great Fire in 1666 – in the diaries of Samuel Pepys and John Evelyn. These should be in your school or public library.

- Below is another poem about London. Read it several times and think about what it means and what is interesting about it. Then introduce the poem to the rest of the class.

'Sunken Evening'

1   The green light floods the city square,
        A sea of fowl and feathered fish,
        Where squalls of rainbirds dive and splash
    And gusty sparrows chop the air.

5   Submerged, the prawn-blue pigeons feed
        In sandy grottoes round the Mall,
        And crusted lobster-buses crawl
    Among the fountains' silver weed.

    There, like a wreck, with mast and bell,
10   The torn church settles by the bow,
        While phosphorescent starlings stow
    Their mussel shells along the hull.

    The oyster-poet, drowned but dry,
        Rolls a black pearl between his bones;
15   The typist, trapped by telephones,
    Gazes in bubbles at the sky.

    Till, with the dark, the swallows run,
        And homeward surges tide and fret –
        The slow night trawls its heavy net
20   And hauls the clerk to Surbiton.

Laurie Lee (1983)

Chapter 8 Drought

The rice harvest

Jinda lives in a rural village in Thailand in the 1970s. A long drought has led to failure of the rice crop upon which the villagers depend.

1   Heat the colour of fire, sky as heavy as mud, and under both the soil – hard, dry, unyielding.

It was a silent harvest. Across the valley, yellow rice fields stretched, stooped and dry. The sun glazed the afternoon with a heat so fierce that the

5   distant mountains shimmered in it. The dust in the sky, the cracked earth, and the
10   shrivelled leaves fluttering on brittle branches – everything was scorched.

15   Fanning out in a jagged line across the fields were the harvesters, their sickles flashing in
20   the sun. Nobody spoke. Nobody laughed. Nobody sang. The only noise was wave
25   after wave of sullen hisses as the rice stalks were slashed and flung to the ground.

30   A single lark flew by, casting a swift shadow on the stubbled fields. From under the brim of her hat Jinda saw it wing its way west. It flew to a

tamarind tree at the foot of the mountain, circled it three times and flew away.

A good sign, Jinda thought. Maybe the harvest won't be so poor after all.
35 She straightened up, feeling prickles of pain shoot up her spine, and gazed at the brown fields before her. In all her seventeen years, Jinda had never seen a crop as bad as this one. The heads of grain were so light the rice stalks were hardly bent under their weight. Jinda peeled the husk of one grain open: the rice grain inside was no thicker than a fingernail.

40 Sighing, she bent to work. A trickle of sweat ran down between her breasts and into the well of her navel. Her shirt was stuck to her in clammy patches, and the sickle handle was damp in her palm. She reached for a sheaf of rice stalks and slashed through it.

Reach and slash, reach and slash. It was a rhythm she must have been born
45 knowing, she thought, so deeply ingrained was it in her.

Out of the corner of her eye, she saw the hem of her sister Dao's sarong, faded grey where once the bright flowered pattern had been. Dao was stooped even lower than the other harvesters in their row and was panting slightly as she strained to keep up.

50 From the edge of the field came the sudden sound of a thin, shrill wail.

'Your baby's crying, Dao,' Jinda said.

Her sister ignored her.

'Oi's crying,' Jinda repeated. 'Can't you hear him?'

'I hear him.'

55 'Maybe he's hungry.'

'He's always hungry.'

'Why don't you feed him then?'

'Why don't you mind your own business?' Dao snapped.

'But couldn't you try?' Jinda insisted, as the wailing got louder. 'I think at
60 least you should try.'

Dao slashed through a sheaf of stalks and flung them to the ground. 'When I want your advice, sister,' she said, 'I'll ask for it.'

They did not speak again for the rest of the afternoon. The baby cried intermittently, but Jinda did her best to ignore it.

65　How different this is from past harvests, Jinda thought. Just three years ago before the drought, she and Dao had gaily chatted away as they cut stalks heavy with grain. They talked about what they might buy after the harvest – new sarongs, some ducklings, and a bottle of honey. And as they talked, the dark handsome Ghan had sung love songs across the fields to Dao, until her

70　face turned so red she had to run down to the river and splash cold water on it.

　　When Dao and Ghan were married the whole village attended the wedding. All that morning the hundred or so families of Maekung each took their turn to tie the sacred thread around the bridal couple's wrists, and after the

75　elaborate wedding feast countless couples, young and old, had danced the Ramwong until the moon rose high above the palm trees and the kerosene lamps were lit.

　　There had been so much of everything then, Jinda thought wistfully, so much food and rice wine, so much music and movement, and, best of all, so much

80　laughter.

　　And now, just two very poor harvests later, there was never any laughter, nothing but the whisper of sickles against dry stalks in parched fields. Ghan had left to work in the city even before their son was born, and Dao – poor Dao, Jinda thought, stealing a glance at her sister's grim face – Dao had

85　become just a shadow of her former self.

　　Slightly abridged from *Rice without Rain* by Minfong Ho (1986)

EXERCISE 8.1

Now answer these questions as fully as you can:

1.　Roughly how many people lived in the village of Maekung?

2.　Why do you think Dao is reluctant to feed the baby?

3.　What does Jinda miss most from earlier years?

4.　Why did Ghan go to the city?

5.　Write a paragraph of your own to describe the traditional Thai rice-harvesting scene in as much detail as you can.

6.　What do the villagers do with the surplus rice crop in a good year?

7.　Why do you think Minfong Ho describes Dao's wedding?

Africa needs emergency aid

This letter was published in the *Daily Telegraph* on 7th July 2011. Described as an 'open letter' it was also published in a number of other places.

1   SIR – East Africa faces the worst food crisis of the century. Livestock are dying, markets empty, food prices rocketing and people starving. Levels of acute malnutrition among refugees fleeing Somalia are some of the highest seen in decades.

5   In Ethiopia, Somalia and Kenya 12 million people are in dire need of clean water, food and basic sanitation. Massive loss of life is a real risk and the crisis is set to worsen in coming months.

While severe drought has led to the huge scale of the disaster, this crisis has been caused by people
10 and policies as much as nature. The global food system is clearly not working.

Five of the past seven years
15 have seen poor or failed rains in the region. The ability of pastoralists to cope with drought has been systematically undermined,
20 as land traditionally used in emergencies has been sold off or allocated for tourism, national parks and large-scale agriculture.

25 Emergency aid is needed right now to save lives and so that people can rebuild once the crisis is over. Oxfam has launched its
30 largest emergency appeal for Africa to raise

£50 million to reach 2.5 million people. It's vital that governments and donors also invest in longer-term support to help people cope with more frequent droughts and to prevent future crises.

35   Laura Bailey
      William Boyd
      Jonathan Coe
      Livia Firth
      Peter Gabriel
40   David Gandy
      Mark Haddon
      Sally Hawkins
      Victoria Hislop
      Lauren Laverne
45   Annie Lennox
      Michael Morpurgo
      Rankin
      Colin Thubron

      Oxfam, Oxford

      Letter published in the *Daily Telegraph* (July 2011)

EXERCISE 8.2

Answer the following questions:

1.   Which three East African countries are affected by the drought?

2.   Who has organised the sending of this letter?

3.   How many people will continue to be in urgent need of help even if Oxfam manages to raise £50 million?

4.   What is/are: (a) basic sanitation and (b) pastoralists?

5.   Why is it now particularly difficult for pastoralists to cope with drought?

6.   What do the people who have signed this letter want to happen?

7.   What do you notice about the names below this letter?

The Ancient Mariner

An old sailor, The Ancient Mariner, is describing his troubled travels at sea in Coleridge's long, famous poem, first published in 1798. The mariner believes – and so do the other sailors – that he has brought a terrible curse on the ship by shooting an albatross, a large white seabird.

1
The sun now rose upon the right:
Out of the sea came he,
Still hid in mist, and on the left
Went down into the sea.

5
And the good south wind still blew behind,
But no sweet bird did follow,
Nor any day for food or play
Come to the mariners' hollo!

And I had done a hellish thing,
10
And it would work 'em woe:
For all averred I had killed the bird
That made the breeze to blow.
Ah wretch! Said they, the bird to slay,
That made the breeze to blow.

15 Nor dim nor red, like God's own head,
The glorious sun uprist:
Then all averred I had killed the bird
That brought the fog and mist.
'Twas right. Said they, such birds to slay,
20 That bring the fog and mist.

The fair breeze blew, the white foam flew.
The furrows followed free:
We were the first that ever burst
Into that silent sea.

25 Down dropt the breeze, the sails dropt down,
'Twas sad as sad could be;
And we did speak only to break
The silence of the sea!

All in a hot and copper sky,
30 The bloody sun, at noon,
Right above the mast did stand,
No bigger than the moon.

Day after day, day after day,
We stuck, nor breath nor motion;
35 As idle as a painted ship
Upon a painted ocean.

Water, water everywhere,
And all the boards did shrink;
Water, water everywhere,
40 Nor any drop to drink.

And every tongue, through utter drought,
Was withered at the root:
We could not speak, no more than if
We had been choked with soot.

Slightly abridged from 'The Rime of the Ancient Mariner'
by Samuel Taylor Coleridge (1798)

Poetry technique: alliteration

The repetition of the same letter or sound, usually at the beginning of neighbouring words, is known as **alliteration**. In the extract from 'The Rime of the Ancient Mariner', 'furrows followed free' (line 22) and 'would work 'em woe' (line 10) are good examples of this.

If you look back at the other poems printed in this book, you will find plenty of examples of alliteration because it is one of the commonest devices poets use.

More important, however, than spotting examples is to identify the purpose and effect of alliteration whenever it is used. Ask yourself:

- What does it add to the music of the poem?
- What does it add to the meaning?
- Would it be a worse poem without alliteration?

Apply these questions to any example you are studying.

(N.B. Notice the wonderful effects Coleridge achieves with internal rhyme (see Chapter 4) in 'The Rime of the Ancient Mariner'.)

EXERCISE 8.3

Read the extract from 'The Rime of the Ancient Mariner' very carefully several times. Now answer these questions:

1. Is the ship heading north or south? How do you know?

2. Why can the ship not proceed?

3. The words (a) hollo (line 8) and (b) uprist (line 16) are archaisms (words no longer in everyday use). Work out their meanings from the poem and explain each of them in your own words.

4. Coleridge's poem is written mainly in four-line verses. Why do you think he uses two six-line verses at this point?

5. Pick two examples of alliteration and explain how the effect of each adds to the meaning of the poem.

6. What do you think the rhyme adds to the poem?

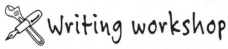 Your turn to write

EXERCISE 8.4

1. Describe any journey you have made on water.

2. Write a story about a community struggling with drought.

3. Write a description of someone suffering from the effects of drought in East Africa.

4. Write a poem about or by someone affected by a drought.

5. Continue Jinda's story.

6. Write about drought in any way you wish.

✏️ Writing workshop

Writing a letter for publication in a newspaper

Most letters which appear in newspapers express a strong opinion and state what changes the letter writer (or writers) would like to see.

The skill is to keep the content of the letter as straightforward as possible and to use very direct language. The shorter the better too.

The letter above about the drought in East Africa:

- indentifies the problem in its first sentence. 'East Africa faces the worst food crisis of the century.'

- uses the rest of the first two paragraphs to explain the extent of the crisis

- explains in the next two paragraphs why this crisis is worse than previous ones

- argues strongly ('Emergency aid is needed right now to save lives') that governments and donors should provide money immediately.

The language is very direct. The letter:

- is only 215 words long

- contains very few adjectives and adverbs

- depends almost entirely on simple and compound sentences rather than longer complex sentences (see Chapter 6 for more on this)

- is arranged in five short paragraphs, each one building on the one before.

Note – it is customary to address letters for publication to the Editor. In traditional newspapers such as the *Daily Telegraph* each of these letters that appears on the letters page will start with 'SIR –'. Some newer or less traditional newspapers and magazines no longer use this convention.

EXERCISE 8.5

Write a letter for publication in a newspaper. Choose a topical subject about which you feel very strongly.

It could be a national issue for a national newspaper or something local relating to your area, home or school (the need for a new road or a pedestrian crossing on a dangerous junction, for example).

Start by checking your facts carefully. The strongest arguments are always based on facts.

Your letter should be 225 words or fewer.

Keep your language as direct as you can.

You will probably need to make several drafts and to edit your work very thoroughly.

These people are protesting against the rise in university tuition fees in the UK, which is an example of a national issue

Grammar and punctuation

Fronted phrases

A basic English sentence usually begins with the subject (**bold** in the examples below), followed by a verb (underlined) after which there may be an object or various constructions (in brackets):

> **Her sister** ignored (her).
>
> **The sun** rose (upon the right).
>
> **People** have (rights).
>
> **I** enjoyed (the poem).
>
> **Jinda** laughed.

However, if a writer shapes too many sentences in this basic way, it makes the writing seem very flat and monotonous. So, to make your writing lively and interesting, you need to experiment with the order of the words (syntax) and to find ways of holding back the subject. Look at these examples:

> Sighing, **she** bent (to work).
> Across the valley, **yellow rice fields** stretched, (stooped and dry).
>
> Day after day, day after day,
> **We** stuck, (nor breath nor motion;
> As idle as a painted ship
> Upon a painted ocean).

In each case the **fronted phrase** – the words which come before the subject – tells you more about the subject.

Each example could be rearranged to put the subject at the front.

EXERCISE 8.6

Write down the three examples above. Then write them again, but this time start each with the subject. Be careful not to change the meaning.

Decide which sentence you think is better – the original one or yours. Be sure you have a well thought-out reason for your opinion.

EXERCISE 8.7

Using the following fronted phrases, write complete sentences by adding a subject, a verb and anything else you wish:

1. Together
2. After the storm
3. For many years
4. Near our school
5. Armed with a broom
6. Puzzled
7, Beneath the flames
8. In the morning light

Hyphenated adjectives

You can be very inventive with adjectives, if you put two words together and link them with a hyphen:

> **Burmese-born** Minfong Ho sets her novel in Thailand.

> Coleridge's **thirst-maddened** mariner has sailed all over the world.

Using an original, hyphenated adjective often means you can express your ideas colourfully but in fewer words.

EXERCISE 8.8

Use your own invented, hyphenated adjectives to complete these sentences:

1. _____ Thailand is in south-east Asia.

2. 'The Rime of the Ancient Mariner' is the longest poem in my _____ anthology.

3. Many _____ tourists visit Bangkok.

4. I am tired of _____ television programmes.

5. Access to _____ water is a basic human right.

6. Imagine our _____ teachers at break, smiling over their coffee.

Spell check: al/ally words, single/double r

Adjectives which end in '-al' add 'ly' when they become adverbs, creating a double 'l'. So:

ironic**al**	ironical**ly**
geographic**al**	geographical**ly**
usu**al**	usual**ly**
practic**al**	practical**ly**

Verbs like 'aver' (meaning 'to state strongly') usually double their final 'r' when they take an 'ed' or an 'ing' suffix. So:

aver	ave**rr**ed	ave**rr**ing
transfer	transfe**rr**ed	transfe**rr**ing
occur	occu**rr**ed	occu**rr**ing

EXERCISE 8.9

For each of the following words, use the correctly spelt '-ed' and '-ing' forms of these verbs in sentences of your own. Write two sentences for each root word:

recur	infer	defer	bar	refer

EXERCISE 8.10

Learn the spelling of these ten words. They are all used in the three passages in this chapter:

agriculture	intermittently	wistfully	tongue	drought
malnutrition	systematically	business	governments	disaster

Vocabulary

Latinate derivations

A 'vulnerable' person is at risk. It is **derived** (comes) from the Latin word *vulnerare*, meaning 'to wound'.

EXERCISE 8.11

Use the following adjectives, all derived from Latin, in sentences of your own. Write in brackets after each one which Latin word it comes from. A good English dictionary will give you this information:

1. culpable
2. hostile
3. pugnacious
4. puerile
5. fraternal
6. caprine
7. belligerent
8. sedentary
9. military
10. veracious

EXERCISE 8.12

In the passage from *Rice without Rain*, Minfong Ho uses the word 'parched' to describe the ground (line 82). How many other words and phrases can you find in the three passages which describe lack of water or extreme heat? Then use a thesaurus, either in book form or on a computer, to see how many more words with similar meanings you can add.

Speaking and listening

1. With your teacher's permission, invite into school a speaker from a charity such as Oxfam to talk to your class about drought in Africa. One of you should introduce him or her and another should propose a vote of thanks at the end.

2. Prepare an assembly about drought.

3. What does 'drought' mean in Britain and how does it affect people's lives? Discuss this in groups.

4. Devise a playlet set in a village in a hot country suffering from drought. Show it to the rest of the class.

5. Prepare a rehearsed reading of the extract from 'The Rime of the Ancient Mariner' printed in this chapter. Perform it as movingly as you can.

Have you read?

The following all feature drought or journeys on water:

- *Rice Without Rain* by Minfong Ho (1986)
- 'The Rime of the Ancient Mariner' by Samuel Taylor Coleridge (1798)
- *The Clay Marble* by Minfong Ho (1989)
- *Pigeon Post* by Arthur Ransome (1936)
- *Holes* by Louis Sachar (2001)
- *The Great Elephant Chase* by Gillian Cross (1992)
- *Life of Pi* by Yann Martel (2003)
- *The African Queen* by C S Forrester (1935)
- The Bible, Genesis Chapters 37–50, for the story of Joseph

 And if you've done all that ...

- Research the albatross. Use reference books or the internet to find out where it is seen, its appearance, food, habitat and breeding. Put your information onto a poster for the classroom wall.

- Construct a timeline for the life of Samuel Taylor Coleridge (1772–1834). Plot on it wars, kings, events, books published, music written, discoveries and inventions made and anything else which interests you.

- Read the rest of 'The Rime of the Ancient Mariner'. Work out – perhaps in a group – how you might stage it as a mime or a play with words.

- Organise a fund-raising event to support a drought-related project.

- Listed below are the jobs of the fourteen eminent people who signed the letter about drought:

Laura Bailey (model)

William Boyd (author)

Jonathan Coe (author)

Livia Firth (ethical designer)

Peter Gabriel (musician)

David Gandy (model)

Mark Haddon (author)

Sally Hawkins (actress)

Victoria Hislop (author)

Lauren Laverne (presenter)

Annie Lennox (musician)

Michael Morpurgo (author)

Rankin (photographer)

Colin Thubron (author)

Choose three – ideally three of whom you hadn't previously heard – and find out more about their work and achievements.

Chapter 9 Bullying

A bully in authority

David Copperfield has been placed at Salem House, a boarding school in London. His tyrannical stepfather, Mr Murdstone, wants him out of the way after an argument which ended in David's biting Murdstone's hand. At school, David is forced to wear a placard on his back which says 'Take care of him: He bites'. This is David's first meeting with the headmaster.

1   The wooden-legged man turned me about so as to exhibit the placard; and having afforded time for a full survey of it, turned me about again with my face to Mr Creakle, and posted himself at Mr Creakle's side. Mr Creakle's face was fiery and his eyes were small, and deep in his head; he had thick
5   veins in his forehead, a little nose and a large chin. He was bald on the top of his head: and had some thin wet-looking hair that was just turning grey, brushed across each temple, so that the two sides interlaced on his forehead. But the circumstance about him which impressed me most was that he had no voice but spoke in a whisper. The exertion this cost him, or
10   the consciousness of talking in that feeble way, made his angry face so much more angry, and his thick veins so much thicker when he spoke, that I am not surprised, on looking back, at this peculiarity striking me as his chief one.

'Now,' said Mr Creakle. 'What's the report of this boy?'

'There's nothing against him yet,' returned the man with the wooden leg.
15   'There has been no opportunity.'

I thought Mr Creakle was disappointed. I thought Mrs and Miss Creakle (at whom I now glanced for the first time and who were, both, thin and quiet) were not disappointed.

'Come here, Sir!' said Mr Creakle, beckoning to me.

20   'Come here!' said the man with the wooden leg, repeating the gesture.

'I have the happiness of knowing your father-in-law,' whispered Mr Creakle, taking me by the ear; 'and a worthy man he is, and a man of strong character. He knows me and I know him. Do you know me? Hey?' said Mr Creakle, pinching my ear with ferocious playfulness.

25   'Not yet, Sir,' I said, flinching with the pain.

'Not yet? Hey?' repeated Mr Creakle. 'But you will soon. Hey?'

'You will soon. Hey?' repeated the man with the wooden leg. I afterwards found that he generally acted, with his strong voice, as Mr Creakle's interpreter to the boys.

30 I was very much frightened, and said I hoped so, if he pleased. I felt, all this
35 while, as if my ear were blazing; he pinched it so hard.

'I'll tell you what I am,' whispered
40 Mr Creakle, letting go at last, with a screw at parting that
45 brought water into my eyes. 'I'm a Tartar.'

'A Tartar,' said the man with
50 the wooden leg.

'When I say I'll do a thing, I do it and when I say I will have a
55 thing done, I will have it done.'

'... will have a thing done, I will have it done,' repeated the man with the wooden leg.

60 'I am a determined character,' said Mr Creakle. 'That's what I am. I do my duty. That's what I do. My flesh and blood,' – he looked at Mrs Creakle as he said this – 'when it rises against me is not my flesh and blood. I discard it. Has that fellow' – to the man with the wooden leg – 'been here again?'

'No,' was the answer.

65 'No,' said Mr Creakle. 'He knows better. He knows me. Let him keep away. I say let him keep away,' said Mr Creakle, striking his hand upon the table and looking at Mrs Creakle. 'For he knows me. Now you have begun to know me too, my young friend, and you may go. Take him away.'

I was very glad to be ordered away, for Mrs and Miss Creakle were both
70 wiping their eyes, and I felt as uncomfortable for them as I did for myself. But I had a petition on my mind which concerned me so nearly, that I couldn't help saying, though I wondered at my own courage:

'If you please, Sir ...?'

Mr Creakle whispered, 'Hah! What's this?' and bent his eyes upon me as if
75 he would have burnt me up with them.

'If you please, Sir?' I faltered. 'If I might be allowed (I am very sorry indeed, sir, for what I did) to take this writing off, before the boys come back ...'

Whether Mr Creakle was in earnest, or whether he only did it to frighten me, I don't know, but he made a burst out of his chair, before which I
80 precipitately retreated without waiting for the escort of the man with the wooden leg, and never once stopped until I reached my own bedroom where, finding I was not pursued, I went to bed, as it was time, and lay quaking for a couple of hours.

From *David Copperfield* by Charles Dickens (1850)

EXERCISE 9.1

Answer these questions as fully as you can:

1. How many people were present at this interview?

2. Who were they?

3. Why do you think Mr Creakle didn't see his new pupil alone?

4. What do you learn about Mr Creakle's wife and daughter from this passage?

5. Give another word which means approximately the same as (a) Tartar (line 47), (b) discard (line 62), (c) faltered (line 76), (d) precipitately (line 80).

6. Who is being bullied? (Think very carefully about this.)

7. Sum up in your own words the narrator's feelings after the interview.

Red Balloon Learner Centres

Carrie Herbert founded a charity called Red Balloon which runs schools for bullied children. This passage explains how it began.

1 In November 1996 Dr Carrie Herbert, a teacher and educational consultant, received a phone call that was to change her life. It was from the parents of a 13-year-old girl called Harriet who had been so badly bullied at a girls-only boarding school that she had taken an overdose. Her parents
5 were asked to remove her from the school.

For six weeks Harriet stayed at home. Then her parents heard that Carrie Herbert ran a school for bullied children in
10 Cambridge. In fact this was not true. At a lecture in Brighton Carrie had indicated that a school was necessary but, at the time, did not exist.

15 However, when Harriet's parents contacted Carrie and told her of their desperation, she invited them to come and see her and to bring Harriet with them.

When they came they told Carrie of their confusion and helplessness and of their horror that their daughter had been so carelessly cast adrift. As
20 they talked, Harriet, a slip of a girl, sat white faced and mute, staring at the floor, her body language indicating defeat and misery.

Seeing their plight, Carrie made an instant and momentous decision. She told the family that she would, indeed, start a school. Harriet would be its first pupil and she could 'begin on Monday.'

25 Within six months Carrie had turned her house into a school, recruited teachers, contacted her local authority who sent her more badly bullied out-of-school children and started the slow process of rebuilding shattered lives.* This was the extraordinary birth of Red Balloon, a charity that runs schools for severely bullied and traumatised secondary school children.

30 By the time that they arrive at a Red Balloon Learner Centre, many of these children have attempted or contemplated suicide. Some are suffering from

post-traumatic stress disorder (PTSD) and have flashbacks, insomnia and panic attacks. Some are speechless with fear and all have low self-esteem.

35 Red Balloon has come a long way since 1996 and several new learner centres are up and running. Through patience, understanding, encouragement and one-to-one counselling the dedicated staff have helped many young people regain trust and a sense of self-worth in a place where they are safe and valued. No Red Balloon Learner Centre takes in more than 15 pupils at any one time and the children know they can remain at

40 the school until they are ready to go back to mainstream education, on to college or into the workplace.

At some time in their lives most people have experienced bullying and know how isolating it can be. It is my hope that the recounting of first-hand experiences by bullied children, and the advice from those who help them,

45 will shed light on this insidious and brutal practice, encourage those experiencing bullying to seek help and give adults – and children – the tools with which to tackle it.

Note:
*At the time of writing Harriet has a responsible job in London. The overdose she took at age 13 long forgotten, she will never forget that first meeting with Carrie Herbert who, quite simply, turned her life around.

From *Rising above bullying, from despair to recovery* by Rosemary Hayes and Carrie Herbert (2011)

EXERCISE 9.2

1. When did the first Red Balloon Learner Centre open and how long ago was it?

2. Explain the meaning of (a) mute (line 20), (b) traumatised (line 29), (c) insidious (line 45).

3. What is the long-term aim of Red Balloon Learner Centre education?

4. Why were Harriet's parents desperate?

5. Summarise in your own words what most bullied children have in common when they arrive at a Red Balloon Learner Centre.

6. How do Red Balloon Learner Centres differ from ordinary schools?

'Ozymandias'

1   I met a traveller from an antique land
    Who said: 'Two vast and trunkless legs of stone
    Stand in the desert. Near them, on the sand,
    Half sunk, a shattered visage lies, whose frown
5   And wrinkled lip, and sneer of cold command,
    Tell that its sculptor well those passions read
    Which yet survive, stamped on those lifeless things,
    The hand that mocked them and the heart that fed;
    And on the pedestal these words appear:
10   "My name is Ozymandias, King of Kings:
    Look on my works, ye Mighty and despair!"
    Nothing beside remains. Round the decay
    Of that colossal wreck, boundless and bare
    The lone and level sands stretch far away.'

Percy Bysshe Shelley (1818)

Poetry technique: consonance

Sometimes poets and writers choose words because they have consonants within them which mirror, match or chime with those in other words nearby. This is called **consonance**.

Consider: 'Half **s**unk, a **s**hattered vi**s**age lie**s**, who**s**e frown' (line 4).

The four similar 's' sounds in the line are an example of consonance. They give the words a hiss of menace.

This is different from **rhyme**, because the consonants can come anywhere in the words, rather than simply at the end. It is different, too, from **alliteration**, which applies to sounds usually at the beginnings of words. Poets often blend rhyme, alliteration and consonance together.

Remember that all these techniques depend on **sound**, not spelling.

EXERCISE 9.3

Read the poem 'Ozymandias' on page 143 and then answer the following questions:

1. Who is the narrator of the poem?

2. Describe the remains of the statue in the desert in your own words.

3. Give a word which means the same as (a) trunkless (line 2), (b) visage (line 4).

4. What interests you about the last three lines of the poem?

5. Why do you think this poem has been included in a chapter focusing on bullying?

Your turn to write

EXERCISE 9.4

1. Imagine you are Miss Creakle. You are writing your diary for the day on which you first met David Copperfield. Add as much extra detail of your own as you wish.

2. Write a story or poem of your own about a child who is bullied.

3. Imagine you are the victim of bullying. Write a letter or email to a teacher setting out your problem.

4. Write the text of a newspaper advertisement for a holiday in Egypt, looking at desert sights (and sites!).

5. Why do people become bullies and how can they be helped? Write your views.

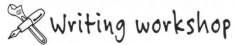 Writing workshop

Writing a sonnet

(Some of you may find this tricky but it is interesting to explore.)

A **sonnet** is a poem with fourteen lines of equal length.

The first sonneteer was Petrarch in 14th century Italy. He devised the form for love poetry. It soon became popular in France and England, and eventually Germany, and was used to express ideas about many subjects as well as love.

Most sonnets use one of two rhyme schemes or patterns.

Many sonnets in English are arranged in two sections – one of eight lines (the **octave**) and one of six (the **sestet**). Wordsworth's sonnet 'Composed upon Westminster Bridge, September 3 1802' which we studied in Chapter 7 and Shelley's 'Ozymandias' in this chapter are both examples of this form. Look carefully at the rhymes of the ends of the lines in these poems to see how the poets have split up their sonnets.

The other form is the one used by Shakespeare. See Chapter 5 for an example. Shakespeare's sonnets have three four-line sections (look at the end rhymes) known as **quatrains** and then end with two lines which rhyme – a **rhyming couplet**.

In English (although other languages use different metres for sonnets) the **iambic pentameter** which we looked at in Chapter 5 is usual.

This makes a sonnet – either sort – a very specific poem to write. Each of the fourteen lines must have five feet and around ten syllables. The ends of the lines must rhyme to conform with one of the two patterns discussed above.

Quite a challenge! Yet many poets have written large numbers of sonnets because they feel very at home with the form.

EXERCISE 9.5

For a learner sonneteer the easiest way to experiment is to write a sonnet closely modelled on one you have read.

Try, for example, writing a Shakespearian sonnet (three quatrains and a rhyming couplet) expressing hate or dislike for someone beginning 'Shall I compare thee to a winter's night.' Make every line a version of Shakespeare's 'Sonnet 18'.

Or model one on 'Ozymandias' (octave and sestet) beginning 'I met a tourist from a foreign place.'

When you feel confident enough have a go at writing a sonnet about anything you wish. A character in Shakespeare's *Henry V* writes a sonnet about his horse, for example. You could write one about a pet, a building, an event, a place or to express strong feelings. Decide before you begin which form you are going to use.

Grammar and punctuation

Fronted clauses

In Chapter 8, we looked at fronted phrases. Here we learn about **fronted clauses**.

The difference between a clause and a phrase is easy to understand. **A clause contains one or more verbs** which have a clear tense (known as **finite verbs**). **A phrase has no finite verb**.

As with the fronted phrases in Chapter 8, fronted clauses are a way of delaying the subject of the sentence and the main verb. They help writers to vary the shapes of their sentences. A fronted clause often needs a comma after it before the main sentence begins.

Look at these examples of fronted clauses. For clarity in the examples, the fronted clause is marked in **bold** with its own finite verb underlined:

Nasty bully as he <u>was</u>, Mr Creakle was probably a coward at heart.

When you <u>are waiting</u> at a bus stop, you don't expect to see the Queen driving past.

After noticing that his watch <u>was missing</u>, Mr Swynford notified the police.

Because I <u>love</u> pears, I bought a whole kilo at the supermarket.

A brave woman who <u>is</u> not afraid to speak her mind, Mrs Smithers angrily confronted the intruder.

EXERCISE 9.6

Complete these sentences by adding a main sentence to the fronted clause:

1. If a teacher makes the lesson interesting, …

2. After Adam had finished his lunch, …

3. An impulsive girl who rarely thought ahead, …

4. Once his prep was given in, …

5. Because I enjoyed *David Copperfield*, …

6. A statue which lies in ruins in the desert, …

EXERCISE 9.7

Add a fronted clause to these sentences. Remember that a clause needs at least one finite verb.

1. … , the bully was sent home.

2. … , Charles Dickens was a prolific writer.

3. … , Mrs Edwards learnt to swim.

4. … , you can't help noticing.

5. … , I enjoyed Shelley's famous poem.

6. … , we all left immediately.

Subordinate clauses

A simple sentence such as 'I like English.' needs no punctuation other than a capital letter at the beginning and a full stop at the end. You can, however, make it more complex by adding **subordinate** (secondary) **clauses**. These are also known as **dependent** (hanging) **clauses**. If you do this, you will need to divide them from the main sentence with commas. Think of the whole sentence as a closed box. Commas can be used only inside the box.

So:

Because I had a wonderful teacher in my school[1], I like English, which gives me huge amounts of pleasure[2], especially when we read classic books[3] that I wouldn't otherwise have known about[4].

Four subordinate statements have been included:

[1]   I had a wonderful teacher in my school. (fronted clause)

[2]   English gives me huge amounts of pleasure.

[3]   We read classic books.

[4]   I wouldn't otherwise have known about (them).

You need the commas to make sense of this complex sentence. They act like signposts.

Words in the mirror

Sometimes in English the word order (syntax) changes the meaning of what is written or said. Simply reversing two words can make a difference. It's like looking at the words in a mirror. And sometimes in the mirror, the two words, as they were once, have come to be written as one. Look at these examples of this kind of 'mirror':

output	put out
upstart	start up
offcut	cut off

EXERCISE 9.8

Use these pairs of words in sentences of your own to show you understand their meaning. Write two sentences for each pair:

1.	income	come in	4.	helpless	less help
2.	upset	set up	5.	outreach	reach out
3.	overturn	turn over	6.	outlook	look out

EXERCISE 9.9

Add as many subordinate clauses as you can to these basic sentences, using commas where you need them:

1.   My school is small.

2.   Dickens wrote many novels.

3. Our headmistress has introduced an anti-bullying policy.

4. Shelley died in 1822.

5. Eat healthily.

6. Mr Creakle bullied David Copperfield.

Spell check: dis- words

The prefix 'dis' is added to the fronts of words to give an opposite meaning. Sometimes, however, the meaning has changed so that the two words are no longer the straightforward opposites they once were. So:

appear	**dis**appear
cover	**dis**cover
connect	**dis**connect
continue	**dis**continue
appoint	**dis**appoint
grace	**dis**grace

N.B. Learn that the 'dis-' prefix has one 's'. So do all the words in this group.

But when the root word already begins with 's', adding the 'dis' prefix produces a double 's'. So:

satisfy	**dis**satisfy
soluble	**dis**soluble
symmetry	**dis**symmetry
seminate	**dis**seminate

EXERCISE 9.10

Check that you know how to spell the ten words below, all of which are used in the passages in this chapter:

ferocious	whispered	determined	antique	traveller
wrinkled	colossal	received	extraordinary	traumatised

Vocabulary

Words from peto

A 'petition' is a request – from the Latin verb *petere*, meaning 'to seek':

'But I had a **petition** in my mind … ' says David Copperfield, meaning that there is a favour he wants to ask of Mr Creakle.

That, however, was 1850. Today the word usually means a written (or, often now, emailed) document, signed by a large number of people demanding action from a government or other authority.

It can also mean a kind of prayer which asks for something and it has a special meaning in law: a 'petition for divorce' is the formal action taken by someone, known as the 'petitioner' who is asking the courts to grant him or her a divorce.

It can be used as a verb too:

The villagers decided **to petition** for a change in the law.

The adjectival form is 'petitionary':

The vicar led us in a **petitionary** prayer.

ped- and pod- words

A 'pedestal' is something which is stood on. It comes from the Latin word *pes, pedis*, meaning 'a foot'.

Several English words use 'ped-' and the Greek equivalent 'pod-'.

EXERCISE 9.11

Look up the meanings of the following words and then use them in sentences of your own:

1.	podium	6.	pediform
2.	quadruped	7.	podiatry
3.	arthropod	8.	pedicab
4.	pedicure	9.	centipede
5.	pedometer	10.	tripod

Speaking and listening

1.   Interview someone over 50 about bullying in schools in the past. Discuss attitudes to bullying today with a teacher at your school and with some other pupils. Write an article on the interview for your school magazine about how attitudes have changed.

2.   Work out a role play with two other people. One of you is a bully and one is a victim. The third person is another pupil or a teacher who stops the bullying. Try this several times so that you each try out each of the roles.

3.   Prepare a short talk for your class about either the novels of Charles Dickens or schools in the 1850s. If you like, and if it is possible, this could be a PowerPoint presentation.

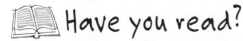 Have you read?

All these books relate to the theme of bullying:

*   *David Copperfield* by Charles Dickens (1850)
*   *Tom Brown's Schooldays* by Thomas Hughes (1857)
*   *I'm the King of the Castle* by Susan Hill (1974)
*   *The Chocolate War* by Robert Cormier (1974)
*   *Fat Boy Swim* by Catherine Forde (2003)
*   *The Bailey Game* by Celia Rees (2002)
*   *Chicken* by Alan Gibbons (1993)
*   *Malarkey* by Keith Grave (2003)
*   *The Protectors* by Pete Johnson (1998)
*   *Finding Jericho* by Dave Jeffery (2008)
*   *A Perfect Ten* by Chris Higgins (2008)

And if you've done all that ...

*   Use the internet and/or reference books to find out what you can about the short but colourful life of Percy Bysshe Shelley.

*   Find the 1964 poem 'The Place's Fault' by Philip Hobsbaum. It's in many anthologies. Read it carefully several times. Make up some questions about the poem and try them out on someone else in the class. Decide whether, if you had been writing this chapter of this book, you would have used 'The Place's Fault' as a passage to study rather than 'Ozymandias' and, if so, why?

Chapter 10 Animals

> ### Rabbits
>
> Hazel is leading his group of rabbits on a long journey to the safety of a new home on Watership Down. Suddenly there is danger.

1   Hazel thought quickly. If the fox were not too close, all they had to do was run. There was woodland nearby and they could vanish into it, keeping more or less together, and simply continue on their way. He pushed through the burdocks.

Para 5   'How close is it?' he asked. 'And where's Fiver?'   S/S

'I'm here,' replied Fiver, from a few yards away. He was squatting under the long briars of a dog-rose and did not turn his head as Hazel came up beside him. 'And there's the fox,' he added. Hazel followed his gaze.   S/S

The rough weed-covered grounds of the combe[1] sloped away below them, a long dip bounded on the north by Caesar's Belt. The last of the setting sun
10   shone straight up it through a break in the trees. The fox was below them and still some way off. Although it was almost directly downwind and must therefore be able to smell them, it did not look as though it were particularly interested in rabbits. It was trotting steadily up the combe like a
15   dog, trailing its white-tipped brush. In colour it was sandy brown, with dark legs and ears. Even now, though obviously not hunting, it had a crafty,

predatory look that made the watchers among the dog-roses shiver. As it passed behind a patch of thistles and disappeared from view, Hazel and Fiver returned to the others.

20 'Come on,' said Hazel. 'If you've never seen a fox don't bother to go and look now. Just follow me.'

He was about to lead the way up the south side of the combe, when suddenly a rabbit shouldered him roughly aside, pushed past Fiver and was gone into the open. Hazel stopped and looked round in amazement.

25 'Who was that?' he asked.

'Bigwig,' answered Fiver, staring.

Together they went quickly back to the briars and once more looked into the combe. Bigwig, in full view, was loping wearily downhill, straight towards the fox. They watched him aghast. He drew near, but still the fox paid no

30 attention.

'Hazel,' said Silver from behind, 'shall I ...?'

'No one is to move,' said Hazel quickly. 'Keep still all of you.'

At about thirty yards' distance the fox saw the approaching rabbit. It paused for a moment and then continued to trot forwards. It was almost upon him

35 before Bigwig turned and began to limp up the north slope of the combe towards the trees of the Belt. The fox hesitated and then followed him.

'What's he up to?' muttered Blackberry.

'Trying to draw it off, I suppose,' replied Fiver.

'But he didn't have to. We'd have got away without that.'

40 'Confounded fool!' said Hazel. 'I don't know when I've been so angry.'

The fox had quickened its pace and was now some distance away from them. It appeared to be overtaking Bigwig. The sun had set and in the failing light they could just make him out as he entered the undergrowth. He disappeared and the fox followed. For several moments all was quiet. Then

45 horribly clear across the darkening, empty combe there came the agonising squeal of a stricken rabbit.

'O Frith and Inlé!' cried Blackberry, stamping. Pipkin turned to bolt. Hazel did not move.

'Shall we go, Hazel?' asked Silver. 'We can't help him now.'

50   As he spoke, Bigwig suddenly <u>broke out</u> of the trees, running very fast. Almost before they could grasp that he was alive, he had recrossed the entire upper slope of the combe in a single <u>dash</u> and bolted in among them.

'Come on,' said Bigwig, 'let's get out of here!'

'But <u>what – what</u> are you wounded?' asked Bluebell in bewilderment.

55   'No,' said Bigwig. '<u>Never better!</u> Let's go!'   S/S

'You can wait until I'm ready,' said Hazel in a <u>cold, angry tone</u>. 'You've done your best to kill yourself and acted like a complete fool. Now hold your tongue and sit down.' He turned and, although it was rapidly becoming too <u>dark to see any distance</u>, made as though he were still looking out across

60   the combe. <u>Behind him, the rabbits fidgeted nervously.</u>

From *Watership Down* by Richard Adams (1972)

Notes:
[1] A short valley or deep hollow

EXERCISE 10.1

Answer the following questions as fully as you can:

1.   What time of day is it and how can you tell?

2.   What exactly did Bigwig do?

3.   What do you learn about Hazel's leadership skills from this passage?

4.   Find expressions in the passage which mean (a) was accelerating, (b) in dismay, (c) untrustworthy appearance.

5.   Explain why Hazel is angry with Bigwig.

Wombat 'the size of a four-wheel drive' found in Australia

Journalists and their readers are always interested in the discovery of new fossils such as this one in Australia.

1   Palaeontologists in Queensland said they had unearthed a virtually complete skeleton of a diprotodon, a giant wombat-like creature known for its massive tusks and tiny brain.

The diprotodon, about the size of a rhinoceros, was found on a remote
5   cattle station in an area rich in the remains of prehistoric megafauna. The discovery of a virtually complete fossil makes it one of Australia's most significant prehistoric
10   discoveries.

"It was the biggest of them all – the biggest marsupial that ever lived on any continent," one of
15   the researchers, Professor Sue Hand, a palaeontologist at the University of New South Wales, told *Australian*
20   *Geographic*.

"It was a bit like a wombat but looked more like a massive, rhino-type beast ... We've found the skull
25   and jaws, as well as most of the rest of the skeleton. It's a really good specimen."

An artist's impression of prehistoric animals which lived in Australia during the Pleistocene. The two largest animals in the background are diprotodon.

The plant-eating diprotodon roamed the country around 2.5 million years
30   ago and became extinct about 55,000 years ago. Scientists believe the species died out because of the arrival of the first indigenous people or climate change, or a combination of the two.

The area, on the Leichhardt River between Normanton and Burketown, has been a trove of giant creature fossils. Palaeontologists have been searching there for more than 40 years and have found evidence of Australian megafauna such as giant kangaroos and giant lizards.

35

Researchers spotted an arm bone jutting out of the ground last year. Further digging revealed it was connected to a shoulder blade and that much of the skeleton was intact.

40

The bones were found alongside the tooth from a giant goanna – a type of lizard – that appears to have become dislodged while feasting on the carcase[1] of the diprotodon.

"At the end of the carcase was a huge tooth of a goanna," a professor of biological science at the University of New South Wales, Professor Mike Archer, told ABC Radio.

45

"In its savage tearing apart of the carcase it must have torn one of its teeth out."

From an article written by Jonathan Pearlman and published in the *Daily Telegraph* (July 2011)

Notes:
[1] This is an alternative spelling of 'carcass'.

EXERCISE 10.2

Now answer the following questions:

1. Where exactly was the wombat skeleton found?

2. Explain the meaning of the words (a) marsupial, (b) palaeontologist, (c) mega-fauna

3. What can you deduce from the passage about the minimum period during which these animals were living in Australia?

4. What two possible reasons are suggested for the animal's eventual extinction?

5. What do scientists think happened to the animal's body after it died and why?

6. Why is this an important scientific discovery?

'The Tyger'

1   Tyger! Tyger! burning bright
           In the forests of the night,
           What immortal hand or eye
           Could frame thy fearful symmetry?

5   In what distant deeps or skies
           Burnt the fire of thine eyes?
           On what wings dare he aspire?
           What the hand dare seize the fire?

           And what shoulder, and what art
10   Could twist the sinews of thy heart?
           And, when thy heart began to beat,
           What dread hand? And what dread feet?

           What the hammer? What the chain?
           In what furnace was thy brain?
15   What the anvil? What dread grasp
           Does its deadly terrors clasp?

           When the stars threw down their spears,
           And water'd heaven with their tears,
           Did he smile his work to see?
20   Did he who made the lamb make thee?

Tyger! Tyger! burning bright
In the forests of the night,
What immortal hand or eye
Dare frame thy fearful symmetry?

William Blake (1794)

Poetry technique: assonance

Assonance is similar to consonance, except that it's the **vowel** sounds which match:

Tyger! Tyger! burning bright

eyes as wide as a football pool

wrinkled lip

I hate a wasted journey

When Blake writes:

In what distant deeps or skies

Burnt the fire of thine eyes?

or Charles Causley writes:

Deep in the sand they silently sank

And each struck a match for the petrol tank.

They are blending rhyme, alliteration, consonance and assonance. Can you see how it works? Remember to listen to the sounds and ignore the spelling.

The Ancient Greeks regarded poetry as a form of music. Do you think they were right?

EXERCISE 10.3

Study 'The Tyger' and answer the following questions:

1. Whom is the narrator addressing?

2. What do you think the poet means by 'fearful symmetry' (line 24)?

3. Why is the lamb mentioned?

4. What is the meaning of (a) aspire (line 7), (b) sinews (line 10), (c) anvil (line 15)?

5. Why do you think the poet repeats the word 'dread' (lines 12 and 15)?

6. In what ways is this a religious poem?

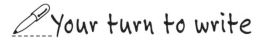

Your turn to write

EXERCISE 10.4

1. Write a factual article for a magazine aimed at young people about the marsupials of Australia. Use the internet as your source of information.

2. Think of an animal which inspires awe, fear, wonder or admiration (or any mixture of these) in you. Write a poem (perhaps a sonnet) addressed to that animal expressing your feelings.

3. Research and write a short biography (really a biographical essay) of William Blake.

4. Write a story in which a group of animals is dealing with conflict.

5. Write about animals in any way you wish.

6. Imagine you are some sort of animal. Tell a story from your point of view.

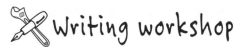

Writing workshop

Animal stories

Stories about animals are usually told in one of two ways:

1. The writer shows the animals only through the eyes of human beings. John Steinbeck's *The Red Pony* and Gavin Maxwell's *Ring of Bright Water* are famous examples of this. Timmy, the dog, in Enid Blyton's Famous Five books is a strong character but always behaves like a real dog.

2. The animals speak, think and live more or less as if they were human beings and the writer takes us inside their world. Beatrix Potter's Peter Rabbit, for example, is really just a little boy who wears clothes, sleeps in a bed and has to be given camomile tea to calm him when he's upset. On the other hand he creeps, every

inch a rabbit, into Mr McGregor's garden to steal vegetables and his father was killed and put into rabbit pie. Richard Adams's rabbits behave very much like human beings, speak a language he calls 'Lapine' (why did he call it that?) and worship a god called Frith – although they sleep in burrows and feed and mate as rabbits would. Or, to take another example, the animals in *The Wind in the Willows* are really human beings. Toad drives cars and lives in a grand house. Mole and Ratty sail in boats and eat picnics.

If you want to tell a story about animals first you must:

- Decide whether your animals will be realistically seen through human eyes or become characters with their own dialogue.

- Work out how many animal and how many human characteristics your characters will have.

- Think about who you are writing for. Traditionally animal stories have usually been meant for children, but *Watership Down* was the Harry Potter of its day. Published initially for children (and winner of the Carnegie Medal for a children's book), it was also read by millions of adults with great enjoyment.

- Think of ways of reminding your readers that these are animals not human beings – otherwise there is no point and you might as well write about people not animals. So you might mention, for example, an animal's tail, snout, eating habits and so on even though he or she is behaving in quite a human way most of the time.

- Make some decisions about dialogue. Will the animals think and speak exactly as if they were human or pepper their speech with, for instance, woofs for a dog or miaows for a cat as a reminder of what they are? Richard Adams invented a language for his rabbits and their speech includes occasional Lapine words to remind the reader that the characters are communicating, but not in human language – which is an ingenious solution.

- Decide, as with any story, whether to tell it as a third person narrative or whether your narrator will be a character in the story.

EXERCISE 10.5

1.   Write a short story about animals in which you present them entirely through the eyes of human beings.

2.   Write an animal story in which the animals have at least some human characteristics.

Grammar and punctuation

Gerunds and gerundives

A **gerund** is a noun formed from a verb by adding 'ing'. So:

> The **going** is tough
>
> Do you like **singing?**
>
> **Swimming** doesn't appeal to me.

A **gerundive** is an adjective (remember they both end in '-ive') formed from a verb by adding 'ing'. So:

> The **parking** space is too small.
>
> **Driving** lessons are fun.
>
> **Cooking** apples are sour.

EXERCISE 10.6

1.   Use the following words in sentences of your own. Write in brackets after each whether you have used it as a gerund or a gerundive:

> eating   playing   walking   shopping   riding   falling

2.   Now write another six sentences using the same words. Where you used a gerund before, now use a gerundive and vice versa. Write in brackets after each what it is.

EXERCISE 10.7

To revise (and test) all the punctuation which you have learnt, write these paragraphs, taking care to punctuate each one correctly:

1. the valley opened out into a great plain dotted over with rocks and cut up by ravines at one end stood a little village and at the other the thick jungle came down in a sweep to the grazing-grounds and stopped there as though it had been cut off with a hoe all over the plain cattle and buffaloes were grazing and when the little boys in charge of the herds saw mowgli they shouted and ran away and the yellow pariah dogs that hang about every indian village barked

    From *The Jungle Book* by Rudyard Kipling (1894)

2. that's polly pig she said pointing to the sow nuzzling the straw in its pen she's mine my dad gave her to me i leaned over the pen yes i know youre a lucky girl she looks a fine pig to me oh she is she is the little girls eyes shone with pleasure i feed her every day and she lets me stroke her shes nice I bet she is she looks nice yes and do you know something else tesss voice grew serious and her voice took on a conspiratorial tone shes going to have babies in march

    From *The Lord God Made Them All* by James Herriot (1981)

Spell check

-al and -le words

Some people confuse words ending in '-cal' and '-cle' because they sound almost the same. Remember that '-cal' words are adjectives and '-cle' words are nouns. Then it's quite easy. For example:

adjectives: '-cal'	nouns: '-cle'
vo**cal**	recepta**cle**
practi**cal**	vehi**cle**
logi**cal**	obsta**cle**

musi**cal**	arti**cle**
physi**cal**	mira**cle**

The same is true of words like 'princi**pal**' and 'princi**ple**' and you need to take special care with them.

N.B. The 'principal' of a college is the principal lecturer, hence the spelling. A 'musical' is a musical entertainment, hence the spelling. In both cases, we are really using a shortened form, which is why the word is spelt as an adjective, although grammatically it's used as a noun.

-ise and -ice words

'advise' is a **verb**:

I advise you to look up the facts.

'advice' is a **noun**:

Mrs Jefferson gave Tim her advice.

This is fairly easy because 'advi**se**' and 'advi**ce**' are pronounced differently in spoken English. 'Devi**se**' and 'devi**ce**' work in the same way.

Use this as a way of helping you to spell correctly a small group of related words which many people get wrong in writing because some of them sound the same in speech:

verbs: '-s-'	nouns: '-c-'
advi**se**	advi**ce**
devi**se**	devi**ce**
licen**se**	licen**ce**
practi**se**	practi**ce**
prophe**sy**	prophe**cy**

Beware of American spelling, which occurs in books published in the USA, in some films and on some websites etc., and does not make this distinction. Nonetheless, it is important that you get it right in British English.

EXERCISE 10.8

Check that you know the spellings of these ten words, all of which are used in this chapter:

particularly	amazement	approaching	fidgeted	professor
skeleton	indigenous	carnivorous	immortal	symmetry

EXERCISE 10.9

Add the correct word ending to each of the incomplete words below:

1. an historic_____ novel
2. the mirac_____ of the loaves and fishes
3. a new bicyc_____
4. physic_____ education
5. Archimedes's princip_____
6. a hysteric_____ laugh

EXERCISE 10.10

Add the correct word ending to each of the incomplete words below:

1. I like to pract_____ the piano.
2. Elijah began to proph_____.
3. I shall apply for a provisional driving lic_____ as soon as I'm 17.
4. Hockey pract_____ is my favourite activity.
5. I must lic_____ my television.
6. There is a lot of proph_____ in the Bible.

Vocabulary

Verbs of movement

The fox in *Watership Down* 'loped'. This is a **verb of movement** like 'ran', 'walked', 'strolled' and 'galloped'. Make a list of as many verbs of movement as you can, writing them down in their past tense, '-ed' form. Try to use some of the less obvious ones in your own writing when it's appropriate.

Words from *spirare*

The verb 'aspire' (usually with the preposition to) means 'to yearn', 'to have a powerful or ambitious plan' or 'to hope to do something':

He aspires to be a great leader.

The related noun is 'aspiration' and the adjective 'aspirational'. They all come from the Latin verb *spirare*, meaning 'to breathe'.

> ### EXERCISE 10.11
>
> Look up the meanings of these related words and use them in sentences of your own:
>
> 1. inspire
> 2. expire
> 3. transpire
> 4. conspire

Speaking and listening

1. Organise a class discussion – or a formal debate – on an animal-rights subject, such as fox hunting or medical experimentation on animals.

2. Comb anthologies for an animal poem which appeals to you. Practise reading it until you feel really confident and then perform it to the class. You might also learn the poem by heart.

3. Prepare an instructive talk about how to care for a pet. (You will have to decide what the pet is.) Take it in turns to deliver your talks in small groups.

4. With your teacher's consent and help, invite in a speaker from one of the well-known animal charities, such as Cats Protection, RSPCA or Dogs Trust. Interview the visitor in groups, having carefully prepared your questions.

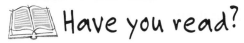 Have you read?

These are all animal stories:

- *Watership Down* by Richard Adams (1972)
- *Encounters With Animals* by Gerald Durrell (1958)
- *Tarka the Otter* by Henry Williamson (1927)
- *Jennie* by Paul Gallico (1950)
- *Blitzcat* by Robert Westall (1989)
- *The White Giraffe* by Lauren St John (2006)
- *Ring of Bright Water* by Gavin Maxwell (1960)
- *Zoo Vet* by David Taylor (1976)
- *The Red Pony* by John Steinbeck (1937)
- *If Only They Could Talk* by James Herriot (1970)
- *Born to Run* by Michael Morpurgo (2007)
- *War Horse* by Michael Morpurgo (1982)

✔ And if you've done all that ...

- As you have seen, in *Watership Down,* Richard Adams's rabbits speak a made-up language called Lapine. Make up some vocabulary for a language called Feline, Canine or Caprine. Remember that you need language only for activities and ideas which affect you. In Lapine, for instance, Adams's rabbits go out at dusk every day to 'silflay' – characteristically rabbity grazing. Humans and other animals don't need a word for this!

The Zebras

1   From the dark woods that breathe of fallen showers,
     Harnessed with level rays in golden reins
     The Zebras draw the dawn across the plains
     Wading knee-deep among the scarlet flowers.
5   The sunlight, zithering their flanks with fire,
     Flashes between the shadows as they pass
     Barred with electric tremors through the grass
     Like wind along the golden strings of a lyre.

     Into the flushed air snorting rosy plumes
10 That smoulder round their feet in drifting fumes
     With dove-like voices call their distant fillies,
     While round the herds the stallion wheels his flight,
     Engine of beauty volted with delight,
     To roll his mare among the trampled lilies.

Roy Campbell (1931)

- Enjoy the poem above (it's a sonnet, of course). It's worth reading several times. Use it as a starting point for your own personal anthology of animal poems. Search published selections and collections. Copy or type out the ones you like and keep them in a notebook or ring binder. D H Lawrence's 'Snake' or John Masefield's 'Reynard the Fox' might appeal to you.

- This book has several times mentioned 'American spelling'. Do you know why it's different from British spelling? Look up Noah Webster and find out.